Employee and Members Assistance Programs Second Edition

I0448484

Employee and Members Assistance Programs
Second Edition

What They Were, What They Are, and
What They Will Look Like in the Future

William Kelly LAP-C, Ph D, C.D.A

Visit www.booksurge.com to order additional copies.

Employee and Members Assistance
Programs Second Edition

ACKNOWLEDGMENTS

Just about everyone has seen Academy Award winners begin their acceptance speech by saying something along the lines of I'm sure I will forget to thank somebody". If there is one certainty it is I will also forget. To those I unintentionally pass over, my apologies and thanks.

When I first began searching for data for my original project, I spoke with an acquaintance of then, over 20 years, Walter Scanlon. His expertise in the field of EAPs along with his own published work gave me a supportive foundation to begin this journey. John and Martha McCaffrey are supportive friends. They are both Ph. Ds. and educators. They helped me to maintain focus on this project. Many thanks Jack and Martha. Mike McDonald taught me how to research. He told me if I wanted to find something, I could. Thank you, Mike. Ben LoCasto and Ted Mapes were also supportive. Ben was the manager of Employee Advisory Services for Met Life while Ted is with the Union Assistance Program for the Transport Workers Union in New York City as well as Past President of the Labor Assistance Professionals, both National and New York City, the founding Chapter of LAP. Ted was also the Labor Chair of the Employee Assistance Professionals. To list all his accomplishments and awards for recognition would not only take up pages, it would, to those who know Ted, embarrass him to no end. Thanks to Henry Spence for his support and for acting as a resource. Henry was also with the Union Assistance Program of the Transport Workers Union and Past President of the NYC Chapter of LAP.

PREFACE

In 1985 I was elected as an official in my labor local. Along with my duties of policing the collective bargaining agreements the local had with its' 2 employers and interacting with management on behalf of the membership, I also handled health and safety issues. Drug and alcohol problems and issues came under the health and safety umbrella. The components of the health and safety quickly separated. On the one hand there were the problems traditionally viewed as health and safety issues. Asbestos, Carpal Tunnel Syndrome, Ergonomics, and other problems remained in the area of health and safety while drug and alcohol problems became a separate entity. Those problems were addressed through a Member Assistance Program. The field of drug and alcohol problems is commonly called Employee Assistance Programs. In my case, as the case with many other unions, the field is referred to as Member Assistance or Union Assistance. These titles serve as notifying individuals of the type of programs available. Within these varying titles lay optional programming such as an internal program or external program. Internal or external programs are exactly what they sound like. Companies and unions can have a program in the workplace or union offices or they can contract the program to an outside provider of such services. My local program was internal as were the programs of both employers.

Eventually, many assistance programs expanded their vision and began to handle problems other than alcohol and/or drug problems. This did not come as a surprise to me. I have been referring members and their families to mental health professionals for assistance in the areas of stress management, depression, and suicide ideation. This was in addition to my assisting in the areas of alcohol and drug problems. The seemingly all inclusive approach is not new to unions. They have a long history of providing a wide range of services to their members and their families. Today, the problems faced by employees and union members are more problematic. Mental health problems, AIDS, along with alcohol and drug problems, and other issues will be discussed in subsequent chapters. The union history of past assistance programs will also be addressed.

In 1995, I decided to find information about the field I had been working in since 1985. I became interested in the past, wondering what early programs looked like and how assistance programs came into existence. There was also a desire to discover if they were truly of value to the employer and to unions. There was a need for me to see if assistance programs had changed with the times. If they did change, what type of changes took place and why they occurred? What were the catalysts necessitating these changes, and were they still of value to labor and management? These two areas of interest tweaked my curiosity. If they had changed, what would they look like in the future and why?

I managed to acquire a great deal of information regarding the past, present, and possible future of assistance programs. Successes and limitations of programs were disclosed. However, the information was not readily available. It was to be found through extensively researching what I was seeking. Since I am not a researcher by nature, uncovering this information took a great deal of time and effort. There really is no single place where this information is readily available. The AFL/ CIO has very little to offer in the way of assistance program data, successes, or failures; likewise, the Employee Assistance Professional Association (EAPA). For that reason I decided to put this information in one place. I managed to find magazine articles about the subjects. These articles came from a cross-section of magazines, not just publications aimed at the fields of chemical dependency treatment or mental health help. Many, if not all the magazines or periodicals I managed to find dealing with these subjects are not mainstream publications. They come from the chemical dependency field, human resources, and business magazines and reports. Additional data was gleaned from books and papers written by educators and professionals in the fields of chemical dependency treatment and mental health care. Much of the newer information is gleaned from the Internet.

Assistance programs are growing in number. They are increasing their areas of assistance. Anyone interested in this research may find this information helpful. Those who want to begin an assistance program be they management, unions, or those who wish to begin external programs with the hopes of offering them to employers or unions will, hopefully, find this material extremely helpful. It is my belief that there is enough information regarding assistance programs contained herein to be viewed as a one stop shopping for employee or member assistance program data. Naturally, this information is not limited to assistance program personnel or those who wish to start programs. Those in the Social Work field or Mental Health Professionals may find this information of value. Many individuals in the latter fields work or desire to work with employees and union members who have problems. Many workers have health insurance. This affords the employee/member access to Social Workers and Mental Health Professionals, while these care givers are repaid for their services. The information provided here will give them an insight to the cultures and histories of both employee and union assistance individuals and programs. The information contained herein is also written for the curious. Some people may be interested in reading about alcoholism, drug addiction, and mental health and their affect on the working person. All too often we believe that these illnesses are the sole province of the unemployed or marginally employable portion of the population. This will show that to be false. In an effort to reach all possible readers, I will use one of A/As' more familiar phrases, "keep it simple". No psycho-babble or words that will have the reader scrambling for a dictionary or thesaurus. Plain talk and verifiable facts are what this is all about.

Finally, the information made available in this presentation may lead anyone interested into further depths of assistance programs. This may not be one stop shopping for all interested parties. It will, however, provide direction toward more in-depth data. For those in the labor field and interested in starting or continuing their programs, I suggest you research the Labor Assistance Professionals. This is an organization specifically dedicated to labor people and their families. It has its' own Certification for Labor Assistance Professionals and a curriculum for teaching course materials necessary to pass the Certification examination. The curriculum is recognized as containing legitimate, approved college bearing credits. Labor Assistance Professional—Certified or LAP-C is the only credential recognized as solely for Labor People. It wasn't set up on a whim. Much thought and preparation went into the creation of this unique certification. Ted Mapes, and many others too numerous to mention worked hard getting this certification recognized and approved. They made sure the LAP-C exam had some teeth, not to be viewed as a walk in the park and took ten years to put in place. Currently the preparatory course is being taught at the National Labor College.

I dedicate this book to three people who were important, people whose brains I picked often and who never seemed to run out of ideas, insight, or the willingness and ability to help. Jack Hennessey, Mickey Diamond, and Greg Monahan. You guys will never need an electric light to read this book. You are basking in a light much greater than any that could be man made.

Of course none of this was possible without the support of my wife of 43 years, Sally and my children Kerry Boynes, Bill Kelly, and Deirdre Atton, and especially my Son-in-law, Ken Boynes, who took on the unenviable task of teaching me how to use a computer.

CHAPTER 1

Doctors usually have a patient history and hopefully a historical knowledge of the illness or disease they are diagnosing and treating. In my opinion the same principle applies in dealing with alcohol and other drugs. How can we deal with the issues of helping our members and their families, and the workplace, if we don't know the driving force behind the issues? It is simple to just say a person is an alcoholic or a drug addict but how far back in our cultural roots does this problem go? We are continually fighting a battle with a substance that has been around since the dawn of recorded history. Some uses were and continue to be useful. Our concerted battle against addictions is virtually embryonic. We can trace some hints against the dangers of alcohol and some attempts to stem the tide of excessive drinking back over two thousand years but for us the real effort surrounding Member or Union Assistance Programs, or Employee Assistance Programs began approximately two hundred years ago. Before starting a program of understanding alcoholism we need to understand alcohol. We need to know our enemy. Huang, (1992) in his interpretation of "Art of War" by Sun-Tsu, reminds us that in order for a mission to be successful we need to understand prior actions.

The Origin and Uses of Alcohol

In my personal presentations on alcohol use and abuse I make mention, somewhat comically, that 10000 years ago Ug left his cave, tripped over a rock and fell face-first into a puddle of fermented water. He arose saying "this stuff is terrible but I feel differently. Not bad, just a little strange. I guess it isn't that bad". Most people don't realize that the observation I made on Ug is at least 10000 years after the fact. Research has shown us that accidental fermentation is at least 20000 years old and probably longer.

Deliberate fermentation is 10000 years old. Discoveries of Stone Age Beer Mugs or jugs dating to the Neolithic Period, 10000BC, tell us that beer fermentation, processed by man is that old ((Patrick, 1952, pp. 12-13). Wine appears as a finished product 6000 years ago, approximately 4000 BC in Egypt ((Lucia, 1963a, p. 216), It has been suggested that beer may have preceded bread as a food staple (Braidwood et al, 1953; Katz and Voigt, 1987). We know that some alcoholic beverages provide nutrients. In countries like Ireland, stout or porter was often prescribed by doctors to increase weight on children and the sickly. Technological advances in food nutrients are prevalent in today's society bringing much needed vitamins and minerals into our fast paced life style, often dictating that our meals be consumed by non nutritious fast foods. Ghaliounqui, (1979) relates that Egyptian bouza and Sudanese merissa long ago contained fats, carbohydrates, and high levels of protein, necessary ingredients in a nutritional diet.

We know from old movies and text that alcohol was popular with the Egyptians as a form of medicine and was an important part of Egyptian culture. Rulers and affluent people were often buried with food and wine for their journey to the next life. Osiris was the God of Wine and was worshiped throughout the region. Ghaliounqui, (1979) also tells us that the Egyptians brewed no less than seventeen varieties of beer and twenty four varieties of wine. Forty-seven hundred years ago the Babylonians worshiped a wine goddess and offered wine and beer as gifts to their Gods.

The Romans and the Greeks of long gone eras had various uses for alcohol. It was used occasionally, copiously, religiously, or celebratory, depending on the rule and life style of the period. Wine making didn't arrive on the Hellenic Peninsula until 2000BC but in a few short three hundred years, it became as common in that area as in the rest of the world used with food, medicinally, religiously. Here we begin to see a different approach to wine and consumption. The Greeks for the most part were quite temperate with their overall wine consumption. Followers of the Dionysian Cult were intemperate a nice description for heavy drinkers, but their consumption was religiously connected. They felt that drunkenness actually brought them closer to their God (Raymond, 1927, p. 55).

The practices of the Dionysian Cult eventually found its way to the Roman Empire. From the beginning of Rome, approximately 753BC to the third century BC, it is believed that, for the most part, Rome and Romans were moderate wine drinkers. Things changed around that time and excessive drinking in the pattern of Dionysian Cult took over. Know as Bacchanalia, it was eventually banned by the Senate (Lausanne, 1969, p. 4; Cherrington, 1925, v. 1, pp. 251-252).

Was this an indication that alcohol was a problem? The abuse of wine in Rome included drinking on an empty stomach, before meals, induced vomiting to consume more wine and food. Some consumption was dictated by the roll of the dice. Excessive drinking was prevalent. Julius Caesar and Cato the Elder were singled out and praised as people of moderation. Before that recognition of temperance, no one had been identified and praised for moderation in drinking. To me, this is an indication that society was recognizing that excessive drinking was out of control. Things didn't get much better for a while. As the Empire decayed, drinking increased and spread. Marc Antony took pride in his destructive drinking. As far back as the third century BC, there was a call for treating the excessive drinker differently from other people. The abuser was recognized as sick but in a different manner, and therefore could not be treated traditionally.

Lutz, (1922) tells us that alcoholism and excessive drinking didn't appear to be a problem for the Egyptians and the Babylonians but both cultures, despite drunkenness not being a criminal act, had warnings on drunkenness, or excessive drinking. This is another indicator that alcohol may cause problems?

As time marched on so did alcohol. There is evidence of alcohol use in pre-historic China. Gernet (1962) and Balazs, (1964) tell us that alcohol was drunk daily around the time of Marco Polo, and that the sale or distribution had to be somewhat controlled by the government in existence at that time since alcohol was a big source of income for the treasury.

Moving on we come to see alcohol in the modern day religions, having roots dating back thousands of years.. Christians have used wine in their religious ceremonies for two thousand years. The Jews were using wine in their religious ceremonies for centuries after having been exposed to wine in Egypt. Eventually wine became a more integral part of their religion and not just for excessive consumption. There are several Biblical references saying wine was a blessing from God and a symbol of joy. Around 525 B.C., it was ruled that the Kiddush (pronouncement of the Sabbath) should be recited over a blessed cup of wine. This established the regular drinking of wine in Jewish ceremonies outside the Temple (Austin, 1985, p. 19).

One of the often told stories in the New Testament is the changing of Water into Wine by Jesus Christ, his first miracle. Religious conviction not withstanding, this is a significant point in history, fact or fiction, since it has serious impact on the future of Christianity. By the late second century there were several heretical sects that rejected the use of alcohol and were calling for abstinence. The early church combated this move through responding that Wine was an inherently good gift from God and was to be used and enjoyed, in moderation and categorized abuse or excessive drinking of alcohol as a sin. Those not capable of moderate consumption were told to abstain (Austin, 1985, pp.44, 47-48).

There is always a nice story connected with alcohol. There is the legend of the discovery of Brandy by Spanish Monks. The legend says they brewed up a really bad batch of wine, so bad it was undrinkable. They distilled it into Brandy. During that time period a single star appeared giving rise to the Hennessy Brandy logo. The first year represented by the single star or comet was good, the second and third represented by two and three stars or comets were even better products. Hennessy went on to Five Stars but the legend of the stars or comets stopped at three.

The Middle-Ages present a different look at alcohol consumption. In the early Middle-Ages, mead, rustic beers, and wild fruit wines became increasingly popular, especially among Celts, Anglo-Saxons, Germans, and Scandinavians. However, wines remained the beverage of preference in the Romance countries what is now Italy, Spain and France (Babor, 1986, p. 11). After the fall of the Roman Empire, there was a decline in urban life. Various religious institutions, primarily Monasteries took over the task of brewing beer and the making of wine. There were still some local beers made outside of the Monasteries but the Monks seemed to have the edge on brewing and brewed most of the good beer until the twelfth century. Around the same time, Ale became popular in England and, along with beer, was used as forms of rent payments to the Lords. Moncton, (1966) relates that by the end of the Middle-Ages, brewing was recognized as a skill and brewers recognized as a guild.

The Black Death or Plague gave rise to drinking for believed health reasons. Some people dramatically increased their consumption of alcohol in the belief that this might protect them from the mysterious disease. The plague, in some instances killed eighty-two (82%) of the residents of a village or town. Some thought that through moderation in all things, including alcohol, they could be saved. It would appear that, on balance, consumption of alcohol was high. For example, in Bavaria, beer consumption was probably about 300 liters per capita a year (compared to 150 liters today) and in Florence wine consumption was about ten barrels per capita a year. Understandably, the consumption of distilled spirits, which was exclusively for medicinal purposes increased in popularity (Austin, 1985, pp. 104-105,107-108).

Many have heard the adage that 'God invented Whiskey to keep the Irish from ruling the world'. History tells us that it really wasn't god's fault. The Irish are actually credited with inventing distilled grain spirits or whiskey, and by the sixteenth century it was widely used in parts of Scotland. Albertus Magnus (1193–1280) is credited with the discovery of the distillation process but it looks like the Irish did it before he wrote down the directions.

During the sixteenth century when John Calvin and Martin Luther were revamping Christianity, the movement of settlers, traders, explorers, adventurers, and those seeking refuge from religious persecution began finding their way to the shores of the New Word, discovered about one hundred years in the past. With them came many of their traditions and these traditions contained the use of alcohol. As the earliest colonists began their new life in the New World, the use of alcohol was already in discussion, and possibly under suspicion. In 1629 the Virginia Colonial Assembly sent a warning to their own religious leaders, saying ""Ministers shall not give themselves to excess in drinkinge, or riott, or spending their tyme idellye day or night," (Cherrington, 1920, p.16). This appears to be a rather ignominious introduction to the religious leadership of Colonial America. Today many consider it proper to 'hang out' in the local bar. Cherrington (1920), Warnings against 'hanging out' are about three hundred and fifty (350) years old. In 1637 the Massachusetts Colony warned that you couldn't hang out in the local tavern longer than necessary. Just a few years earlier, the Plymouth Colony had prohibitions on the amount of money that could be spent on 'spirits', setting two pence as the limit unless you were welcoming newly arrived strangers. Are these signs of early warnings of the dangers presented by excessive alcohol and attempts to limit the use and sale of alcoholic beverages?

Seventeenth Century America also saw the Virginia Colonists continue the traditional belief that alcoholic beverages are a natural food and are good when used in moderation. In fact, beer arrived with the first colonists who considered alcoholic beverages essential to their being (Baron, 1962).

The Puritan Minister, Increase Mather, preached in favor of alcohol but against its abuse: "Drink is in itself a good creature of God and to be received with thankfulness, but the abuse of drink is from Satan; the wine is from God but the Drunkard is from the Devil" (Rorabaugh, 1979, p30).

During that same time period, the first brewery in the colonies was established on Staten Island, NY, later be known as Richmond county, a county in the city of New York (Rouche, 1963). The cultivation of hops began in Massachusetts and brewing and distilling were not just encouraged in Maryland but was to become legislatively encouraged (Austin, 1985).

Some colonists were obviously worried about the excessive use of alcohol by their fellow colonists and maybe even concerned about the health of the indigenous Native Americans, who had never previously been exposed to distilled spirits. Lee (1963) presents the picture of the pragmatism of the Puritans in maintaining their supply of alcohol. The irony in their warnings is that upon departure from the European Shores, the Puritans put on board fourteen (14) tons of water for the tip. In contrast, they carried forty two (42) tons of beer and ten thousand (10000) gallons of wine. Prohibitions and Temperance will be discussed later.

Summary

This was just a brief look into alcohol, its uses and support for its use throughout history. We saw the good, bad, and the apparently logical reasons for the use and manufacturing of alcoholic beverages. You can't fight an issue unless you know the origin.

CHAPTER 2

This chapter will deal with the history of alcohol abuse in the American workplace with a few, hopefully, interesting examples in other parts of the world. The text will cover pre-Revolutionary America to the present day. We will also look back through previous history to see how alcohol was used to motivate and control. It will show how the view toward drinking in the workplace has changed over time. Examples will be given to show that drinking in the workplace was often encouraged either intentionally or unintentionally. Drinking as a method of defying the rules will also be discussed. The history of substance abuse and the manipulative use of alcohol to benefit a particular person or group will not be a complete history. There will, however, be enough information to indicate that the problem has a long and destructive history and when carefully administered, a big profit maker.

Drinking in the Workplace

Long before the Discovery of America we see examples of alcohol being used as a tool of motivation as well as a celebratory beverage and religious drink.

We need look any further that the military of the modern world, Beer rations are quite common for the troops and the Navy of the United Kingdom has not, as of yet, canceled it's rum ration policy in the Royal Navy. Alcohol has long played a part in the art of war and been an important part of the military life.

The use of alcohol as a method of improvement, reward, or gain was not unique to America. As early as approximately 400 B. C. E., alcohol was used as a tool to avenge an outrage

committed against a citizen of Siena by a member of the
Etruscan ruling class. Arnus, a citizen Clusium was incensed
that his wife was seduced by Lucumo, a member of the powerful
Etruscan ruling class. Arnus' influence was no match against the
influence of Lucumo and his family. He didn't have the political
clout or the ability to mount much of an Army to seek revenge.
He did, however, come up with a unique plan.

> Arnus needed a greater force than he could muster. He
> thought he found the answer in the Celts, who had already
> advanced close to Chiusi....He seems in particular to have
> delivered wine to them, a beverage they loved immoderately
> and which was quite new to them for their own regions
> produced only beer. Aruns used wine as his weapon. He
> brought some to the Celts 'to entice them', in other words
> presumably to show them that the Clusium area had a
> particularly fine vintage (Herm, 1975, p. 8).

The end result was the sacking of Rome. The Celts traveled
as far as Rome and laid siege to that city. They did not capture to
capitol area but did severe damage to the city during the siege.
They eventually were bought off for gold. All this was started
because of wine. Alcohol was used advantageously by Arnus.

History's most famous early conqueror was undoubtedly
Alexander the Great of Macedonia. Previously, it was mentioned
that the Greeks enjoyed their wine but for the most part,
disdained the overindulgence of wine. Not so Alexander the
Great and his conquering army. The Macedonians, unlike the
Greeks, viewed excess use of alcohol as a sign of masculinity and
Alexander himself was believed to be heavy abuser of alcohol,
as was his mother a follower of the Dionysian Cult. Was alcohol
a big part of the victories of Alexander? We might never know.
Being in possession of alcohol induced bravado might explain
the fearlessness of the Macedonian troops. At the Battle of
Gaugamela, the Macedonians were vastly out numbered. The
estimated size of the Persian forces were between 250000 and
500000 with other estimates of one million to Alexander's army

of approximately 40000, formidable odds against a well trained and experienced army but somehow Alexander and his forces won the battle. Did alcohol give them a feeling of superiority? The Celts who chased the Roman Army back to Rome were a rag tag group of loosely connected tribes or clans but they managed to defeat the largest army of that time. As reported to be a historical fact, wine was used as a weapon. Why not alcohol as a similar motivator for Alexander? We saw that it was a successful motivational tool for Aruns.

The Early American workplace and drinking.

We make a huge leap from the fourth century BC to the late eighteenth-early nineteenth century USA in seeing how alcohol was used as a motivator or for increasing profit ethically or unethically.

In the eighteenth century the practice of condoning the use of alcohol was not just limited to Native Americans. In the colonial era of American History the consumption of alcoholic beverages was an integral part of the everyday operations of the American work setting. The motivation differed somewhat. The basic principle of maximizing profit was there and because of that drinking on the job was not only allowed, it was encouraged. Bacharach, et al (1994), refer to these issues in their citations on the Colonial American workplace. Employers and employees believed that beer and ale helped preserve the health of the worker. It was also believed that the consumption of these beverages provided the workers with the energy needed to work (Rorabaugh 1979). Drinking on the job also helped form a bond between the master craftsman and his apprentice (Wilentz 1984:53-54). A kind of brotherhood was created by those who both played and worked together (Johnson 1978:56).

Drinking was a method of communal bonding. It began to come under attack in the latter part of the 18th century. By 1811 workplace drinking began to come under attack from the religious community. The attack was brought on by Dr. Benjamin Rush, referred to as the father of American psychiatry

and Anthony Benezet, a wealthy Philadelphia Quaker. Rush and
Benezet will be discussed later.

The Native American is probably one of the most shameful
examples of the use of alcohol for profit. Lives and cultures were
destroyed for the purpose of maximizing profit.

If anyone remembers the John Ford classic western trilogy
of Rio Grande, Fort Apache and She Wore A Yellow Ribbon,
this scene from Fort Apache may be recalled. I am not speaking
of the Henry Fonda led charge into the apparent trap. I refer
to his ordering John Wayne to destroy whiskey that had been
clandestinely shipped to the reservation, packaged as Bibles,
for Indian consumption. In that particular scene the fact that
the Indian Agent was cheating the Apaches on the weight of
their beef ration was brought out along with the corruption of
the Bureau of Indian Affairs, whose agents increased misery
on reservations ad generated hostility. Although the scene
if fictitious the fact that the Bureau of Indian Affairs did not
provide fairly for the Native Americans and knowingly allowed
the distribution of whiskey to the Native Americans is well
documented. In Rio Grande, John Wayne leads the cavalry in a
daring rescue of children held captive by rampaging Apaches. He
wisely waits until just before dawn, when they are all drunk and
passed out, before leading the charge. Other movies depict the
various tribes as violently disposed because of alcohol. They are
shown falling of their horses as a result of drinking. They traded
anything for whiskey and were cheated. These depictions refer
to problems barely one hundred years in our national past. The
fact is, the problems Native Americans have with whiskey are
much older. One hundred years before the time period depicted
in these movies, alcohol was taking its toll on the eastern tribes
and profit was the motive for distributing whiskey to those
tribes. Native Americans could not handle alcohol. There are
varying opinions as to why they seem to have a problem of more
intensity than other races. Some may say it is genetic. Others
may say that they have only been exposed to hard liquor for a
little over 300 years and have not yet built a tolerance equal to
that of the white man who has been consuming hard alcohol

for centuries longer. The bottom line is they have a problem and others used that problem to their advantage. The problem did not go unnoticed. Some early Native American leaders attempted to stem the tide of alcohol abuse by their fellow tribesmen. They even formed policies that could be broadly viewed as assistance programs.

Alcohol was a problem in the workplace of the Seneca Indian. The Seneca Indians, a tribe of Native Americans and part of the Iroquois Federation led a communal life style. "Economic security for both men and women lay in proper recognition of one's obligation to family, clan, community, and nation, an in efficient and cooperative performance on team activities, such as working bees, war parties, and diplomatic missions" (A. Wallace, 1972, p. 24). "...that they farm a little and make houses; but that they must not sell anything they raised off the ground, but give it away to one another and to the old people in particular in short that they must possess everything in common" (A. Wallace, 1972, p., 281).

Anthony Wallace (1972) devotes a great deal of his book to a Seneca Federation Chief, named Handsome Lake and his bout with alcoholism both on a personal level as well as on the tribal level. Handsome Lake was considered a prophet among the Seneca and as a prophet condemned the vices of white society. Among the vices was whiskey. He preached and wrote against whiskey. In 1799, a Seneca council refused to allow any alcohol into their settlement. By 1803 Handsome Lake received praise for being primarily responsible for curing the Seneca of the misuse of alcohol. He preached temperance and spirituality, similar to the tenets of Alcoholics Anonymous. Handsome Lake created a code, aptly called the Code of Handsome Lake. In this code he spoke out against many things, including alcohol, calling drinking evil (A. Wallace, 1972, p. 241).

In the case of the Seneca, workplace substance abuse stemmed from the influence of an outside source. The Seneca, along with many other tribes traded their communal goods of meat, animal skins or pelts. The pelts were of prime interest to the white trader. Pelts were exchanged for metal knives, pots, and hatchets. A potpourri of articles including rifles, powder, and lead were available for trade. So was whiskey. Occasionally a hunter would give his pelts for rum. This often lead to a hungry family which was depending on the hunter to trade for things that would be of use to his family (A. Wallace, 1972, pp. 24-25).

The Seneca had a propensity for alcohol, as did many other Native American tribes. Through ignorance on the part of the Seneca and with deliberation on the part of the white man, we can see how alcoholic problems manifested themselves in the workplace of the Native American. He was susceptible to the effects of alcohol and the white man took advantage of that susceptibility. The profit motive took on an even more savage appearance than just exploitation. The white man did not care what happened to the Native Americans.

And the people liked to drink. They preferred not to drink alone but in large convivial groups. In the Spring, hunters took their peltries to Warren, got drunk by the scores, and brought more liquor home with them...Bringing liquor back to the grant, returning travelers sold the whiskey at retail and buyers threw all-night parties where, plied with liquor, groups spent whole nights singing, dancing, drumming, and quarreling. Women could be seen after such routs, lying in stupor beside the paths to their homes. And in the late morning the sodden households woke sometimes to find a member dead, or cut in a brawl, or frozen in the snow outside (A. Wallace, 1972, pp. 193-194).

The Seneca were not the only tribe at that time to fall prey to whiskey and have a spokesperson preaching against the evils of liquor. The Delaware were affected and they had their own prophet, Neolin, "the Enlightened." Neolin preached repentance and gave instructions on how to regain the favor of the Creator.

"...Hear what the Great Spirit has ordered me to tell you! You are to make sacrifices, in the manner that I shall direct; to put off entirely from yourselves the customs which you have adopted since the white people came among us; you are to return to that former happy state, in which we lived in peace and plenty, before these strangers came to disturb us, above all, you are to abstain from drinking their deadly *beson* [poisonous, bewitched "medicine," i. e., liquor], which they have forced upon us for the sake of increasing their gains and diminishing our numbers....(A. Wallace, 1972, p. 120).

It is quite possible that Handsome Lake may have indirectly heard of Neolin, the Delaware Prophet (A. Wallace, 1972, pp. 117 &121).

The communal life of the Native American can be viewed as a workplace, as it indeed was. A picture is painted here regarding the white man's allowance of whiskey being made available to a people, in the work place, who were susceptible to its effects. It appears that the use of alcohol in the work place of the Native American was condoned and condoned openly. Alcoholic beverage consumption was used to relieve the Indians of their goods for as little cost as possible. It was not uncommon to find whole Native American towns indulging in periodic sprees of drunkenness. Many of these sprees were brief. Chronic alcoholism took its' toll on the Delaware in the early part of the 18th century. They lost their lands. Native American leaders of that period were ignominiously identified as drunkards. So pervasive was the problem, those leaders who avoided drunkenness were noted as exceptions (A. Wallace, 1972, p. 199). Another bit of irony. We have already seen where Julius Caesar and Cato the Elder were singled out for being temperate at a time when drunkenness was taking its toll on the Roman Empire but excesses were not addressed. Only moderation was given notoriety.

The problem appears to have been addressed in a simple fashion. Abstinence from alcohol was preached. Both Handsome Lake and Neolin abstained and offered themselves as powers of example. There was also the possibility of improving the life style of an individual as well as the family. Things would get better. These principles, developed in the late 18th and early 19th centuries are also part of the tenets of modern day AA. Since both Handsome Lake and Neolin were leaders of their respective factions, they might possibly be categorized as managers. In that vein, their program served their purpose by benefiting their workplace and their tribal members.

Handsome Lake has moved from relative seclusion to a position of some notoriety today. Robbie Robertson, a former member of The Band, an extremely popular band of the 60s and 70s has recorded a song about Handsome Lake. After almost 300 years, Handsome Lake is still remembered, rescued from obscurity.

The post-Revolutionary period saw Americans arriving in the Northwest Territories. There, the actions were the same. White traders took advantage of the Native American proclivity toward alcohol. Again, the profit motive.

> Of all the goods the fur traders brought in their baggage, the most destructive by far was alcohol. To the Indians, firewater, was a magical potion that brought dreams resembling the much-sought-after visions. They would happily exchange a whole season's gathering of pelts for a bottle or two of rum...But it was rum and whiskey that became a primary means of suborning the Indians in order to seize their lands...Every means was employed, from flattery to force, to get the Indians to yield up vast stretches of their domain, and liquor eased the pangs of negotiations (America's Fascinating Indian Heritage, 1978, p. 153).

Let's not forget the importance of alcohol in our political history and how people may have used it to their own advantage. According Eric Burns (2003), the Minute Men, who were called to action at short notice, congregated in bars, probably awaiting news of mobilization. Thomas Jefferson is supposed to have written parts of the Declaration of Independence in a tavern with a glass of wine next to the ink he was using. George

Washington lost his first attempt at the being elected to the Virginia Assembly because he didn't supply enough alcohol to the potential voters. Two years later, after supplying 144 gallons of various alcoholic beverages he won his first election. We saw this practice continue in later elections where elections were bought and paid for by money and alcohol.

The farming industry of the nineteenth century did not escape the problems of alcohol abuse. The farmers were giving their employees, the farm hands, alcoholic beverages, on the job. Alcohol consumption was condoned by the farmers just like it was condoned by the employer in the colonial era along with the master craftsman. The move to keep farmers from freely giving alcohol to their employees and probably manufacturing alcoholic beverages lead to one of the Temperance Movements in the United States. Again, Temperance Movements will be addressed later but for now, we can look at some of the reported or believed benefits to Temperance in the workplace. The obvious gain to the farmer is he would get a better, more productive employee. His crops, he was assured by Rush and Benezet, would be harvested more rapidly. These two obvious gains were supplemented by the fact that he would not have to buy or spend time manufacturing distilled spirits. The farmer saved all around and the employee kept his job.

The problem seems to be that what was being championed as the saving of the worker and the workplace, the disuse of spirits, other industries still provided alcohol to the employee. Moving on in virtually the same time period we see problems and actions against alcohol in the workplace. Bacharach, et al (1994) cite several instances regarding actions against alcohol in the workplace. The temperance leadership was going all out against alcohol in the work place in the 1820s. While they were trying to get people to abstain from alcoholic beverages on the job, they were trying to get the employers to get their workers to abstain off the job as well (Rumbarger 1989). During this time period, the goals of Rush and Benezet were becoming a reality. The farmers were adopting no drinking on the job policies. While this movement against drinking in the workplace was going on the Erie Canal was being built. Workers on the canal were given a wage and a ration of rum.

England, during the 17th and 18th centuries was also using alcohol to its advantage. They had a surplus of grain and used the flooding of cheap gin to raise revenue. At the beginning of the 18th century Parliament actually passed legislation encouraging the use of grains for distilling spirits. They had a public policy that wanted the flooding of the market with cheap gin. This coincided with the fact that there was very little stigma attached to being drunk. It was also a way to give relief to the growing urban, poor population having difficulty facing the everyday realities of urban life. This began what became known as the Gin Epidemic. Parliament passed legislation in 1736 limiting the sale of gin to quantities of less than 2 gallons. By the middle of the 18th century, gin consumption had dropped from 18 million gallons, consumed by a population of 6 million, to less than 2 million gallons. The decline was attributed to increased corn prices and taxes which impacted on the price of gin. Gin drinking became stigmatized and a criticism of drunkenness emerged, along with a ban on distilling. Contributing to the decline of gin consumption was the emergence of a higher quality of beer (Hanson, 2005).

Covert and overt drinking in the workplace of today.

There is what appears to be the overt condoning of the use of alcohol in the work place. We have already seen how drinking on the job was viewed as a method of bonding between employees in earlier times. There really does not seem to be much difference from Colonial times to the workplace of today. The bonding and camaraderie of the Colonial times is still with us. It just goes by different names.

There is another condoning, albeit covert and possibly not deliberate, policy of permissible use of alcohol in the workplace. Many companies sponsor soft ball teams and leagues. Bowling leagues and teams are often sponsored. Employees play either against or with managers on the company or factory teams. Quite often, after and sometimes during these games, alcohol is used, and used by both managers and employees. There are the annual company picnics with similar scenarios. Food and drink, including alcohol, are shared. There are often celebrations surrounding the closing of business deals. There is what is often jokingly referred to as the three Martini lunch. Around the holiday season of Christmas, we see many office parties where alcoholic beverages along with food are served. On these occasions, the food and drink are often paid for by the managers or the company. These are the same people who set the no drinking policies in their respective industries.

That employers who condone and even encourage drinking by employees can be held liable was found in a decision of the California Supreme Court. That court ruled that the employer was culpable in the death of an employee who died in an automobile accident. The employee became intoxicated at the office holiday season party. The festivities were held on company time. The court ruled that an employer who not only tolerates but encourages drinking in connection with the job cannot assert that the accident was caused by the employee being intoxicated (Kinney & Leaton, 1978, p. 255).

Kinney & Leaton (1978) feel that there is a universal presence of alcohol in the work place. They admit that there has not been a study conducted in that area, but they did present a theory.

> The Kinney-Leaton Law states that alcohol will be conspicuously present at any social gathering composed of people who know one another primarily from work. As a corollary, people who may not associate drinking with social gatherings of friends, family, or neighborhood folk will choose to drink as a social function that is tied to work. It would seem that being initially ill at ease as social gatherings, which is a common feeling, might be more threatening if the function consists of co-workers. And alcohol is often used to lessen anxiety. On the other hand, drinking with co-workers may be considered "time out"; co-workers may be far more tolerant of one another's getting a little "tanked" than they would be if the drinking were

being done with spouse, family, or close friends (Kinney &
Leaton, 1978, p. 254).

Several years later their theory received some validation.
In The Seventh Special Report to the U.S. Congress on Alcohol
and Health (1990) it was stated that despite cultural and
social backgrounds being contributing factors to workplace
drinking, other reasons also existed. Workplace characteristics,
permissiveness of the workplace environment, and work related
social issues also contributed to workplace drinking (Ames and
Janes 1987).

To intimate that the permissible use of alcohol in the
workplace is the sole reason for the problems related to chemical
dependency in the work setting of today would be ludicrous.
To say that the pervasive use of alcohol in the workplace was
exacerbated by managers and employers has some validity, as
noted. On the other hand, it would be grossly unfair to place
all the blame for chemical dependency problems in the work
place solely of the shoulders of managers and employers. Some
responsibility must be assigned to the employee, although some
of their reasons for drinking on the job differ from the covert or
overt consent of management. Some people drink in the work
place in defiance of management.

> In many occupations, drinking has remained a badge of
> working-class status and opposition to hierarchical control
> by management. Railroaders (Mannello and Seaman
> (1979), police (Man Maanen 1986), mariners (Molloy 1989),
> longshoremen (Mars 1987), and construction workers
> (Riemer 1979), for instance, still regard drinking as evidence
> of conformity to, rather than deviance from, occupational
> norms. Members of these occupations are *expected* to
> drink with one another on and off the job (Cosper 1979)
> (Bacharach, et al, 1994, p. 9).

The major difference in these examples is that expectation
to drink on and off the job came from the workers themselves.
They needed no prodding or blessing from management. They

would defy the rules. The aforementioned groups also pose a different view from factory or office workers. They could be virtually unsupervised for periods of time. A train crew could go a full day without management on board. A police officer could go through a shift without seeing a supervisor, especially if he or she worked in assignments out of uniform.

Sandhogs.

Naturally, this is not an indictment of the men called sand hogs. I use these men as a prime example of example of why and how drinking is carried on in the workplace. Workplace drinking, as we have seen is not relegated to the construction industry.

Some of the defiant behavior is culturally driven as exampled in looking at a particular group of construction workers who proudly refer to themselves as "sandhogs." A sandhog digs tunnels but is not to be confused with being a miner. They work in a different atmosphere from traditional miners. They often work in areas called "high air," working, quite often, beneath rivers and other bodies of water. High air is an area of compressed air that requires the workers to adjust their bodies both before entering and subsequent to leaving the tunnel or hole. Their work is demanding, hard and dangerous, well paying, and sporadic. They depend on their coworkers for safety and companionship. Their drinking is traditional, stemming not only for the camaraderie of their job but from their heritage. Many of the sandhogs are Irish or of Irish descent. The combination of drinking miners and the fact that theirs is a heritage of Irish drinking the sandhogs create their own subculture in the world of construction. In the world of sandhogging, sometimes it is advantageous to be a drinker, given their history. Sandhogs control the hiring process. This is quite unique in the world of managers and workers.

There is a basic work unit in sandhogging called the gang. The gang is an extremely important piece of sandhogging life. The sandhogs are heavily unionized which is also important in relationship to who and who does not work. "Contractors bid for and win contracts, but it is the union that hires and fires workers. On every tunnel job, there is a walking boss and a foreman who make sure the contractor's orders are fulfilled but who are themselves union members" (Sonnenstuhl & Trice, 1987, p. 230). A union member can not be fired by another peer union member. This provides a safety net for the alcoholic. The thing that will stop him from working is that he is not hired in a gang. The gang is an integral part of sandhogging. Often groups of sandhogs will congregate at the job site in a building called the hog house. There they eat, play cards and drink before, between, and after shifts. If a person is not working that particular shift, he may remain in the hog house, drinking.

Peer pressure will dictate who will and who will not work. In the dangerous world of sandhogs, they do not want to work with an unsafe person. "Although the foreman does the hiring and firing, it is the gang members in evaluating the day-to-day performance of workers who exercise control. If gang members for, instance, believe someone is lazy or dangerous, they will not recruit them" (Sonnenstuhl & Trice, 1987, p. 231). There is an antithesis here. The bar scene is a familiar place to find sandhogs. They use their neighborhood bars as bulletin boards and hiring halls. The fact that the work is sporadic was mentioned earlier. In order for a sandhog to hear the latest news about job possibilities, he must stay in contact with his peers and that location is usually the bar. Unless he is on the site of a job when a person is needed, he will not get the job. The bar is where he will get the information (Sonnenstuhl & Trice, 1987, p. 233). The irony is that although a safe worker is needed, the only place one may find a qualified and possibly relatively safe worker is in the bar.

Workplace drinking; different country: a brief overview.

The issues surrounding the origins of workplace problems are not unique to the United States. The docks of Aberdeen, Scotland are a fine example of drinking on the job. "The fact that from 7 a.m. to 5 p.m. most people on the docks are drinking and working did not seem to cause concern" (Harvey, 1989, p.

102). Company foreman would neglect to enforce safety rules on the docks. These are the same managers who would take a worker out of the local pub. In order to make up the proper number of personnel needed on the docks for a particular job, the foreman would knowingly use an intoxicated worker (Harvey, 1989, p. 104).

I had the opportunity to study labor and alcohol related problems in the United Kingdom in 1989. Regarding alcohol in the work place I personally saw pubs in local Police Stations where off duty officers could enjoy, after work, alcoholic beverages at reduced prices. I also observed a fully operational pub and restaurant, open during business hours and serving anyone of age who entered, on the grounds of a hospital. The possibility that a medical technician, responsible for maintaining crucial equipment, having a few drinks while working scared me. I did not want to think about a doctor having a few shots or a pint or two before he began surgery. There are certain cultural differences between the United Kingdom and the United States. Those cultural differences are not the focus of the study. The focus regarding the U. K. is that drinking on the job, in some circumstances, is condoned.

Retrospectively looking at the dock workers in Aberdeen, Scotland and the sandhogs of America, there appears to be a paradoxical approach to hiring. In the dangerous work on the docks of Scotland, and the perilous work site of the tunnel, no one wants an unsafe worker. We have seen, however, managers and unions willing to hire workers who have been drinking. Both parties are aware of the problem but both appear to willfully over look the issue. Again, the bottom line appears. The managers need a full crew to load or unload the goods on the docks or in the holds of ships while the union's bottom line is keeping people working. The sandhog may garner information concerning a job in the drinking arena, but as has been shown prior, the hiring is done by the walking boss or foreman, both union members.

Summary

So far we have seen how alcohol and addiction to alcohol can be used to serve various purposes. Arnus used the desire of the Celts for a better grade of alcoholic beverage to show the ruling class they could not get away with trifling with those holding positions of less importance. One of the vagaries of history, of which Arnus had no reason to believe would take place, was the Celts fought not only the Etruscans but their Roman allies and eventually sacked Rome. For all intents and purposes the pay for the Celtic services was wine. This is an early example of people using alcohol to serve their own ends at the expense of others.

In America, there was a similar approach. The white man used alcohol to profit from the Native American propensity toward alcohol. The motive of plying the Native American people with alcohol appears to be purely profit as evidenced in the examples supplied. Alcohol led to problems in the communal workplace of the Native Americans and caused them to lose their ancestral home lands. They lost and the white man gained. Alcohol was the catalyst. The Colonial period sees alcohol being used in a more beneficial light. It was believed alcoholic beverages like beer and wine helped ward off illness and built camaraderie between workers. While, on the surface, this appears benign, profit was still the motive. Happy, healthy, and closely knitted employees would work better. Farmers supplied alcohol to their workers until Rush and Benezet came on the scene. There is no reason to believe the farmers' approach to drinking was not similar to the more traditional colonial workplace. No one would supply alcohol or any other substance to employees knowing the substance would negatively impact on production. They did it for profit. Only when Rush and Benezet convinced the farmers their employees would be more effective without alcohol, did they accept their opinion. Rush and Benezet did not just single out farms as workplaces needing to reform their alcohol policies. By the 1820s, temperance leaders were trying to convince all employers to prohibit drinking both on and off the job. A short time later, by the 1840s, the Good Intent Stage Line and the Utica and Schenectady railroads adopted an even sterner policy. They refused to hire anyone who drank alcoholic beverages.

Today, despite looking at the past, we still see alcohol in the workplace. Sometimes it is used openly and sometimes in defiance of rules and regulations. Often it is difficult to see drinking in the workplace. However, it is still there.

CHAPTER 3

As the chapter heading suggests, this part will deal with the impact of alcohol, drugs and mental health problems as they relate to the workplace. We will see just who the substance abusers are and how many of them are out there. Included here are the definitions of an alcoholic and a drug addict. If you are interested in researching numbers in regards to cost to the workplace resultant of alcoholism and drug abuse, and how many alcoholics, and drug addicts are working, here it is. Welcome.

The impact of alcohol abuse, drug addiction, and mental health problems on the worksite.

We can, once again, go back to the movies. In the late 1960s it was fashionable to repeat the phrase from Butch Cassidy and the Sundance Kid. The phrase was "who are those guys", referring to the posse chasing them. We can paraphrase that into "who are the drunks, drug addicts, and persons with mental health issues." We know they are there. We just do not know who they are.

Who are they and how many of them are there?

The alcoholic, the drug addict, or those persons suffering from certain types of mental illness are not as readily identifiable as we may believe. Many people have an indelible image of an alcoholic as one who stumbles down the street, is unshaven and dirty, often begging for money, and living in a cardboard box. Many believe that drug addicts live and hide in burnt out apartment buildings and support their habit through a life of crime, receiving public assistance, or are in some type of penal institution. On the contrary; the Federal Government tells us that 65% of drug users earn in excess of $25,000 annually. We view those suffering with mental health problems as persons who have a distant look about them or constantly mumble to themselves. Nothing could be further from the truth. Certainly, some fit into these categories but not most. Alcoholics, drug addicts, and those suffering from mental illness wear judicial or clerical robes. They invest our dollars, repair our computers, our cars, or our telephones. They teach our children and fly our airplanes. They are Police Officers, Fire Fighters, Doctors, and Nurses. They are everywhere. They sit next to us in our houses of worship and they are in our families. They look and quite often act regular. It is hard to distinguish them from "normal" folks.

In the late 1970s it was estimated that there were 9 million alcoholics in the then estimated population of 200 million people. Of those 9 million, ninety-five percent were employed or employable. They made up five percent of the nation's work force and approximately ten percent of the executives (Kinney & Leaton, 1978, p. 22). By the 1990s there were 10.5 million Americans exhibiting symptoms of alcoholism and alcohol dependence. Approximately three percent of problem drinkers live on skid row or exhibit skid row life-styles. Ninety-seven percent of problem drinkers were living normal lives and could be found in the workplace. An estimated 10.5 million workers are either alcoholic, in some state of alcoholic dependence or using illegal drugs. Seventy percent of illicit drug users were employed. They constitute 10.1 million workers (Scanlon, 1991, pp. 6-7). By 1997 it was estimated that 71% of all drug users were employed with the majority holding down full time jobs (Boles, Aug. 1997, p. 22).

By 1995 it was estimated that there were 111 million persons 12 years and older drinking alcohol. Approximately 32 million engage in binge drinking while 11 million were classified as heavy drinkers. 60% of drinkers were aged 21 through 44. Almost thirteen (12.8) million persons were using illicit drugs. The highest rate of drug users was 18% and was in the age group of 18 to 20 years. 60% of illicit drug users range in age from 21 to 49 (Preliminary Estimates From the 1995 National Household Survey on Drug Abuse, 1996, pp. 10, 20-21).

Cost of Substance Abuse to the workplace

The cost of alcoholism and the abuse of other drugs is nothing new in the American workplace. In 1971 the economic cost associated with alcohol misuse and alcoholism was in excess of $25 billion, with lost production and health and medical costs accounting for $17.64 billion of that amount (Kinney & Leaton, 1978, p. 23). The costs have risen dramatically since that information was compiled. Bacharach, et al (1994) made several citations regarding the costs and escalation of costs caused by alcohol problems. They cite (Rice, et al, 1990) the article "The Economic Costs of Alcohol and Drug Abuse and Mental Health: 1985". In that article they estimated the economic cost of alcohol related problems at $85.5 billion in 1988. In another citation Bacharach, et al (1994) referred to the National Institute on Alcohol and Alcohol Abuse, 1990 "Seventh Special Report to the U.S. Congress on Alcohol and Health". That report predicted that by 1995, the cost of alcohol related problems would reach $150 billion.

While Kinney & Leaton (1978), along with Bacharach, et al (1994) provide figures related to alcohol use alone, Scanlon (1991) cites a (Research Triangle Institute's March, 21, 1990) report on updated costs from a 1983 study. This study includes other drugs, along with alcohol. The government sponsored Research Triangle Institute study showed that lost productivity at that time was in excess of $99 billion annually, with an additional $17 billion being spent on treatment and other support services. By the mid 1980s alcoholism, drug abuse and personal problems, were reported as causing New York State to lose in excess of $8 billion dollars business annually (Pontius, p. 1). The magnitude of such vast amounts of money may be better viewed if it is looked at differently. These reported annual figures equate to combined costs of $318 million daily or more succinctly calculated at the rate $13 million an hour. Pontius provides support for the claim of this study that alcoholism and drug abuse are costing industry millions of dollars in losses. Later in the study The EAP Manual serves as a source for supplying data on the cost of alcoholism and drug abuse to specific industries and companies.

A paper by Nancy K. Young, Ph. D., UCLA School of Public Policy and Social Research also looked at alcoholism and drug addiction. The data used was collected in 1980 and adjusted for 1990. The estimation is that by 1990 there would be 17.5 million people having substance disorders. Approximately 6.1 million people had both a mental disorder as well as a substance use disorder. Dr. Young, in 1985, estimated the cost of alcohol related problems to be $70.3 billion and the cost of other drug problems to be at $44.1 billion. By 1990 the cost of alcohol and other drug use would cost $165.5 billion. This figure translates into a cost of $900 for every adult in the United States, per year (Young, 1994, pp. 5-6).

The government of the United States reports that the number of illicit drug users aged eighteen and over is 71%, and they are employed. The estimate is they make up 5.4 million full time and 1.9 million part time workers. In a study conducted by the U. S. Postal Service, they compared the work performance of its drug using employees against non drug using employees. Drug users had an absenteeism record of 66 percent higher than non drug users while their utilization of health benefits was 84 percent higher in dollar terms, than the non drug users. There were more disciplinary actions and a higher employee turn over rate in the drug users (National Drug Control Strategy, 1997, p. 17).

The U.S. Department of Labor estimated that lost time, accidents, health care, and workers' compensation derived from drug use in the work place cost employers $75 billion to $100 billion. Substance abusers use their medical benefits at a rate 16 times higher than non-abusers. They file workers' compensation claims 6 times more often than the non-abuser. On-the-job accidents related to drug and alcohol use are reported to be 65% of all on-the-job accidents (Bahls, 1998, p., 82).

The overall cost of illicit drug abuse is estimated to have been $160.7 billion in 2000, and 69 percent of these costs are from productivity losses due to drug-related illnesses and deaths. Reducing substance abuse positively impacts America's economic report. Light and moderate drinkers cause 60 percent of tardiness, absenteeism and poor quality work as a result of alcohol consumption. Heavy drinkers and alcoholics cause the remaining 40 percent. Up to 40 percent of industrial fatalities can be linked to alcohol abuse and alcoholism. Thirty-eight percent to 50 percent of all workers' compensation claims are related to substance abuse (National Council on Compensation Insurance). In 1997, workers who reported heavy alcohol use were about twice as likely as those who did not report such use to have worked for three or more employers in the past year. Eighty percent of drug abusers steal from their workplaces to support their drug use. Substance abuse is the third leading cause of workplace violence. Drug-using employees are 3.6 times more likely to be involved in workplace accidents and five times more likely to file a workers' compensation claim. (National Drug-Free Workplace Alliance, 9/05)

Substance abuse is not the only cause for concern. Stress is causing a problem in the workplace and it is expensive. Scott Wallace (1997) reported that stress was costing US business between $15 and $300 billion dollars annually. This was based on a 1992 Industry Week report. Handron (1994), reports that stress is costing the American workplace $200 billion annually. Costs are rising in the areas of cumulative mental stress. Stress-related claims have risen 700% during the 1980s, in California. These claims account for 15% of all workers compensation claims. The Northwestern National Life Insurance 1991 study reported that almost 72% of survey respondents said they experienced some type of stress-related mental condition. These conditions could cause increased health costs. Geber (1996) reports stress as surpassing the common cold as America's number one health problem. Stress related illness cost $100 billion with an additional $17 billion in production losses. Schiff

(1997) says stress accounts for 12% of unscheduled absences and is responsible for costing US businesses $200 billion annually. Even though there has been a period of economic growth, falling unemployment, and low inflation for 7 years, stress levels have increased. Twenty-five percent of employees admit to a great deal of pressure (Stone, 1997).

Coopers and Lybrand report that, in 1990, the country spent $42.4 billion on mental health care. Private insurance paid almost 45% of the money. This does not include the cost in relationship to work related costs. They believed that, as that time, depression was costing the workplace an estimated $44 billion annually. Of that amount, 55% of the losses were attributed to the areas of lost productivity, absenteeism and other factors that present a difficulty in measuring (Gemignani, 1996)

The number of persons in this country that are afflicted with chemical dependency is quite high. When the overwhelming majority of their numbers are known to be in the workplace, this brings the problem into a new area. It is no longer a social problem. Chemical Dependency, along with illnesses like depression that are often linked with chemical dependency, has become major problems in the workplace. The figures and data reported in the study bear out that unfortunate but very real fact. It cost industry entirely too much to have these conditions continue.

There are other reasons why business and industry began to assist employees with drinking problems. Bacharach, et al (1994), said that large companies sponsored assistance programs as an effort toward pacifying workers and to keep them from joining unions. The first Workmen's Compensation was passed in 1908. Worker's compensation laws held employers legally responsible for job accidents.

Before going any further, it is my belief that, to understand the problem, we should go back and look at the causes, real or imagined, of substance abuse in the workplace.

Alcoholic and Drug Addict.

Not everyone who drinks is an alcoholic and not every person who uses illegal drugs is a drug addict. The person using illegal drugs is breaking the law. The alcohol consumer of legal age is not breaking the law. Driving under the influence of alcohol or driving while intoxicated is against the law. A person may run afoul of the law by committing an act of violence or other crime as a result of drinking. What is the difference between these people and those categorized as alcoholics and drug addicts?

An alcoholic is one who suffers from the disease of alcoholism. Alcoholism has several definitions. "Alcoholism is considered a chronic illness of undetermined etiology with an insidious onset, showing recognizable symptoms and signs proportionate to its severity", (The Merck Manual, 1987, p. 1479). Etiology is the cause or origin of diseases. That definition of alcoholism was upgraded a few years later.

> "Alcoholism is a primary chronic disease with genetic, psychological, and environmental factors influencing its development and manifestations. The disease is often progressive and fatal. It is characterized by continuous or periodic impaired control over drinking, preoccupation with the drug alcohol, use of alcohol despite adverse consequences, and distortions in thinking, most notable denial" (National Council on Alcoholism and Drug Dependence [NCADD] and the American Society of Addiction Medicine [ASAM], 28th NCADD Conference, 1990).

The difference in these two definitions lies in identifying alcoholism as a disease. The former says it is the cause of disease while the latter says it is a disease. There really is not much of a difference in the definitions of addiction.

> Addiction refers to a style of living that includes drug dependence, generally both physical and psychological, but mainly connotes continuing compulsive use and overwhelming involvement with a drug. Addiction additionally implies risk of harm and the need to stop drug use, whether the addict understands and agrees or not (The Merck Manual, 1987, p. 1476).

The definition of addiction to alcohol or other drugs have a commonality. They both indicate harm and show the person involved does not or chooses not to recognize the problem and danger. In my opinion, the best and most clearly understandable definition of an alcoholic, drug addict, or as they are often referred to in the language of today, a chemically dependent person, may be the one proffered by Tony N. Tony is well known in AA in the north-east. He is a substance abuse counselor, regional speaker of notoriety, and teacher of counseling techniques. He describes a substance abuser as an individual whose use of alcohol and/or drugs negatively impacts on the persons' home, job, health, or safety, and continues using drugs or alcohol (Personal communication, Feb., 1986). The choice of drugs and/or alcohol is commonly referred to as the drug of choice. The chemically dependent need fit only one category, not all four.

There are two other categories of drinkers that should be mentioned. They are binge drinkers and heavy users of alcohol. A binge drinker is described as one who has five or more drinks on the same occasion in the same day. This should occur at least once in the past 30 days. On the other hand a heavy user of alcohol is one who has 5 or more drinks on the same occasion on 5 days within the last 30 days. I will not speculate or go into a long dissertation on who is and who is not an alcoholic. If a binge drinker or person who is a heavy user of alcohol falls into the category described by Tony N., so be it. At the very least persons who might be categorized as bingers or heavy users may want to evaluate their drinking and subsequent events surrounding their drinking. Any one who has attended AA meetings should be able to recall the stories of people who said they only drank on weekends. For years these people did not believe they were alcoholics.

The binger or heavy drinker may the persons who some believe can be taught to control their drinking. There is a move on in the US to reach out to people who drink too much but say they are not alcoholics. This movement believes in getting the drinker to modify his or her drinking. In 1989, I met with John

Teller, the Director of Avon Council on Alcoholism in Bristol, G.B. They were already moving ahead with the controlled drinking experiment. The significance in mentioning bingers and heavy users of alcohol in the same context as alcoholics and drug addicts is quite clear. Looking at the text book definitions of an alcoholic and the definition offered by Tony N., we find one glaring omission. Not one of the three offered definitions of alcoholism or an alcoholic mentions how much was consumed, when, where, why, or how it was consumed. The relevance of it all lies in what happens when the person drinks or what happens if he or she does not get the drink.

I recall a story of a high ranking television executive, in a television interview on alcoholism and alcoholics. He stated his habit was to have a few drinks at a bar close to the office. One evening at the usual time, having his usual drink, his secretary called him at the bar. She reminded him that he had a late appointment. The executive told his secretary to call the other person, make his apologies and set up another date. The executive returned to the bar and picked up his drink. Before taking another sip, he placed the drink back on the bar and called his secretary back. He asked if she had made the cancellation. She said no. The executive asked her to call the party and tell him he would be late but he was on his way. He left the bar and went on to his meeting. He never drank alcohol again. The television executive went on to explain that he had never once in his entire life been drunk but he realized that alcohol had almost kept him from making a business meeting. Remember Tony N. Home. Health. Job. Safety. Only one component is necessary.

One more drinking classification needs to be mentioned, the social drinker. There are those who seldom drink. They may have a cocktail before a meal once a week and maybe a glass of wine with dinner. They may have a beer with lunch while working around the house or the yard on the weekend. When attending a wedding or similar function, they may have a glass of champagne and a beer or mixed drink. They rarely think about an alcoholic beverage. In no way does alcohol affect any of the four areas spoken about earlier.

A case could be made to find categories like binger and heavy user of alcohol in the world of other drugs, like cocaine, heroin, marijuana, and other drugs. The one major restraint is they are all illegal. If you use one gram of cocaine or one pound, it is still illegal. The same applies in comparing a social drinker to what is called a recreational use of drugs. There may be such a category. I said earlier that not every person who drinks is an alcoholic or every person using drugs is an addict. If alcohol is a drug and people use alcohol sensibly, for its therapeutic value, then why can we not use illegal drugs, sensibly, for their therapeutic value? There may be recreational users of illegal drugs just as there are social drinkers. Again, the key word is illegal. The big problem I have with recreational drug using is in dealing with crack. I have never come across a recreational crack user. I have come across several individuals who experimented once or twice with alcohol and other drugs. The affect of the drugs was so traumatic they never again drank alcohol or took other illegal drugs.

Are Things Getting Better?

Things don't appear to be getting any better. They are getting worse. According to the National Institute of Health (NIH) (2004) the number of adults abusing alcohol or alcoholic has risen dramatically. The study from 1991−1992 indicated that there were 13.8 Million people or 7.41 percent of the population in varying stages of alcohol abuse or addiction. In the years from the NIH study to the new study in 2001−2002 the number jumped to 17.6 million. This reflected in an over 1 percent increase to 8.46 percent. In other words there are, not only numerically more people with alcohol problem but the percentage has also risen. While the population has risen to an all time high of approximately 275 million, up from the approximate 200 million in 1970, the number of those reported to be alcoholic has more than doubled from the 1970 figure of 9 million alcoholics to over 18.6 million people needing treatment for varying degrees of alcohol dependency. A position paper from Brown University, (2000) states that more than one half of all adults have a family history of alcoholism or heavy drinking.

The largest testing laboratory in the country, Quest, reports that, recently, Methamphetamine use rose 68%, showing up in 3 out of 1000 tests; marijuana comes up in 3 or every 100 tests. There is also a slight increase in opiate use.

The loss to companies in the United States due to alcohol and drug-related abuse by employees totals $100 billion a year, according to The National Clearinghouse for Alcohol and Drug Information, while in Canada The Alberta Alcohol and Drug Abuse Commission has estimated the annual cost of workers absent or tardy due to substance abuse to be approximately $400 million just in Alberta alone. Remarkably, much of the losses to industry are not limited to the alcoholic or drug addicted line worker. According to Substance Abuse in the Workplace, (2006),

> "Managers have their share of problems as do casual drinkers. Remarkably, new research shows it is the social drinkers—not the hard-core alcoholics or problem drinkers—who are responsible for most of lost productivity, according to a Christian Science Monitor article, specifically tying the hangover issue to production in the workplace. This study also found that it was managers, not hourly employees, who were most often drinking during the workday. Twenty-three percent of upper managers and 11 percent of first-line supervisors reported having a drink during the workday, compared with only eight percent of hourly employees. The study also found that 21 percent of employees said their own productivity had been affected because of a co-worker's drinking".

The National Household Survey of Drug Abuse (4/2/04) relates; of all those admitted and treated for substance abuse in 2001, 34% were employed at the time of admission, and were more likely to report that alcohol was the primary subject of abuse. Those reporting for alcohol treatment were more likely to be employed than the unemployed seeking treatment for the same problem. Here is a sad twist; the admissions for treatment of the employed came more frequently through the criminal justice system than the unemployed referrals. The percentage is alarming. Sixteen percent of the employed in treatment came through the criminal justice system referrals compared to just 6% for the unemployed. Even more disconcerting is the fact that the number of unemployed admitted for treatment by virtue of self or individual referral was 10% higher than the employed. The common denominator here is that both the unemployed and employed referrals were extremely similar in age, 35 and 36 years of age. Does this tell us of the importance of maintaining or creating EAPs, and Member or Union Assistance Programs?

The number of abusers in the workplace hasn't shown any improvement. In some cases it is worse than 10 years ago. The National Household Survey on Drug Abuse (9/6/02) provides these alarming figures. In 2000 there were 87,672,000 Americans between the ages of 18 and 49 employed as full time workers. Alcohol dependence or abuse was reported by 7.4% for the previous years and drug dependence or abuse was reported by another 1.9% over the same time period. This comes to slightly under 10% of the workforce over 8,150,000 active full time workers and we have not even mentioned the other workers aged 50 to 62 or 65. I believe we can readily see that the figures are still comparative to the 10% mark of alcoholic or chemically dependent workers from the study conducted in the mid. Of the over 87 million workers, 14,822,000 were in some form of managerial capacity, including executive. Another 13,329,000 were employed in technological and sales support, with an additional 13,222,000 employed in the field of Professional Specialties.

Later we will see information not solely about one particular group of workers, like sandhogs, a traditionally a hard working—hard drinking group of men, but about the rest of the construction industry? The same report indicates that almost 11% of those involved in construction or mining are either dependent or abuse alcohol while an additional 3.6% have drug dependency or addiction problems. In real numbers of the

8,267,000 mining and construction workers, almost 950,000 are in some form of addiction or dependency. Many trust their savings to bankers, money managers, stock brokers, others in the financial world and others involved in our recreational activities and lives. The report states that out of the 8,320,000 employed in those areas, some 750,000 are dependent or abuse alcohol and drugs. Even more alarming is the number of professional services employees who are comprised of over 19 million of the 87 million workers. More that 1 million of these employed individuals admitted to having alcohol and or drug abuse or dependency issues in the year of the study.

Not only do we see the need for the establishment of and the continuance of Assistance Programs, we see where they are needed in what may be termed as the less traditional work place. White collar abuse and addiction is on the rise.

Estimates come and go. What most estimates have in common regarding alcohol and other drug problem in the workplace is the cost to the workplace never seems to go down. Often the estimated projected costs are low as exampled by the article on "The Substance Abuse Costs to Society & the Workplace High". Alcoholism costs the workplace 500 million workdays per year. The report reveals a startling new figure. An aggregate accounting of casual drinkers show they account for more absenteeism, tardiness work performance than the person who is alcohol dependent.

The US Department of Health and Human Services (2003) report on substance abuse or dependence provides alarming rising figure. Over 7 million people (7.7) or 3.3% of the population of the US ages 12 and over needed treatment for diagnosable drug problems while 18.6 million or 7.9% of the population needed treatment for serious alcohol problems. We saw earlier that the prediction of those, over 12 years of age drinking alcohol by 1995 would be 111 million people. This latest figure tells us that over 15% of those reported or estimated to be drinking are in need of treatment. Of the drinking population at the time of the report, 54 million were classified as binge drinkers and 15.9 were classified as heavy drinkers.

Current illicit drug use is highest among young adults 18 to 25 years old, with over 20 percent using drugs. Youth ages 12-17 also are significant users, with 11.6 percent currently using illicit drugs. Among adults ages 26 and older, 5.8 percent reported current drug use. There were also 9.5 million full-time workers, 8.2 percent, who used illicit drugs in 2002. Of the 16.6 million illicit drug users ages 18 or older in 2002, 12.4 million were employed either full or part time. Since 1993 those treated for a primary problem for heroin abuse was 195,865. By 2003 the number went up to 272782. Some may ask "why is that important to Member/Union Assistance Program personnel? Just under 67% of those undergoing treatment for heroin addiction in 2003 compiled an average age of 36 years. Cocaine treatment in 2003 rings a similar bell. Almost 250000 were people treated for cocaine dependence and their average age was approximately 35. In 1993, 20,776 people went for treatment with methamphetamine as the primary drug. By 2003, that number has skyrocketed to 116,604 with an average age of 31. These are our people, working people who need our help. If similar numbers reflected the millions of Americans having died as an immediate result of cancer, there would a national cry for helping stem the tide of that destructive disease. MAPs and EAPs are the people carrying on this fight. Twenty years ago there were an estimated 10 million drug abusers and addicts in the workplace. Today the number is reported to be 9 million. The problem is that the number of alcoholics in the workplace has risen dramatically and the indicators are that the numbers of young people soon to be entering the work force are already having difficulty with alcohol and drug abuse.

Times have changed. Marijuana is still the most commonly used illegal substance but second place has been taken over by non medical use and abuse of prescription drugs. An estimated 6.2 million people, 2.6 percent of the population ages 12 or older, were current users of prescription drugs taken non-medically. Of these, an estimated 4.4 million used narcotic pain relievers, 1.8 million used anti-anxiety medications (also known as tranquilizers), 1.2 million used stimulants and 0.4 million used sedatives. The survey estimates that 1.9 million persons used OxyContin non-medically at least once in their lifetime.

The studies reported here are based on ages from 12 on up. Currently it is 2006. The studies were conducted a few years back. The 12 year old population is approaching 16 while the 16 years old population is not 18 to 20 and many are already in the workforce.

We, the people who have been in the field for decades, see a different attitude toward different drugs. There were always different names for alcohol or drugs. Some of those names may escape us but there are newer drugs with newer and different names with a totally different agenda. Twenty years ago few in this country ever heard of Hill-Billy Heroin, or OxyContin; snowbirds were people escaping the wintry north. Now, a snowbird is another name for cocaine. In the streets of New York City, if you hit a ball on a roof, it was a roofie. Today a ruffie (same pronunciation), or roofie, is a date rape drug Rohypnol. Ketamine is a date rape drug; GHB, called Georgia Home Boy or Grievous Bodily Harm is a date rape drug. Unfortunately, many of the women who are victimized by date rape drugs are unaware of the event at the time of occurrence. When they realize what has happened they often become traumatized. Many of them are our sisters in the workplace, whose only crime may have been just 'going out with the girls'.

The list of names and uses of these fairly newer drugs is large and would require pages of description. You can check at: www.drugfree.org/drug.guide/BySlang.

The information available is staggering, giving almost 150 names, many new to the traditional field of alcohol and drugs. Descriptions, uses and complications of using these drugs, inclusive of alcohol, are contained on that site.

Hopefully the words 'skyrocketing' and 'staggering' got your attention because it is probably much worse. Most indicators or surveys conducted today, especially in the governmental surveys already and still to be mentioned, there is a glaring hole in the statistics. Like advertising today, aimed at the younger generation, the older generations, 50 and older, are pretty much ignored. The same goes for the workplace surveys. One of my favorite saying is "liars figure and figures lie". I believe this has never been more evident than in the reporting of workplace alcohol problems and the workplace in general. The statistics are based on the ages 18 to 49. What happened to all those over 50 to 65 and some even older still in the workplace? Did they all disappear? We know that people, those that so afford, are retiring at an earlier age but everyone over 50 is not counted? Wouldn't they impact the numbers for or against treatment or workplace dependency problems? Just look at your own family and possibly yourself. How many people in your family or friends are over 50 and still a viable member of the workforce?

How many have problems with chemicals. How many of us know the 50 and 60 year old 'flower children' of the 60s or even those left over from the 'beatnik generation' of the 50s who are still smoking marijuana?

Summary

We have seen that those suffering from chemical dependency and mental illness are not isolated in the old stereotypical view. They are in our workplace, our community and our homes. They are increasing in number. The National Drug Control Strategy (1997) reports fewer people trying cocaine but heroin addiction surpasses the addiction rate of the 1970s and 1980s. The numbers of those frequently using marijuana are dropping while there is an increase in the use of methamphetamine. The cost to the American workplace as a result of problems stemming from chemical dependency is alarming and rising each year. We have seen how alcohol impacted the work site. We then saw the dramatic increase in cost when the inclusion of drugs other than alcohol, along with alcohol, was entered into the equation. Next we saw the impact of mental health problems in relationship to negatively impacting the workplace. Scanlon (1991) states that of the amount paid by companies for medical coverage, mental health coverage costs were estimated at slightly below 10%, up to 25%. Failure to deal with the problem could lead to double or tripling indirect costs. These are costs affecting the efficiency of a company.

Defining alcoholism and drug addiction becomes tremendously important if there is a decision to help those afflicted with chemical dependency or mental health problems. It would be difficult to address and hopefully solve a problem if the problem or problems had not been identified.

The binge drinker and the heavy user of alcohol were looked at. The difference between them and the alcoholic was spelled out. It is important to note that maybe there is not any significant difference between alcoholic and alcoholism when they are compared to bingers and heavy users of alcohol.

We spent time looking at the newer numbers of alcoholics and drug addicts in society as well as the workplace. Marijuana is still number one on the chart of illegal drugs. Like heroin, it has increased potency. A little goes a longer way or a more intense high. OxyContin was developed as a pain killer intended for the use of people who might not have readily available medical facilities or doctors in their immediate often remote areas of residence. It is easily ground into a fine, granulated powder, easily inhaled. What many in the field of drug addiction asks why, with the technology available, is the manufacturer of OxyContin not doing more to ensure the effectiveness of the medication while making is much harder to break down into a powder like substance, leading to abuse and addiction to prescription meds?

The use of date rape drugs is growing and affects the lives of many women. As a rule, rape is the least reported crime against women. What we need to recognize is that date rape is happening much more often than reported. Ask yourself; if a woman is reluctant to report a violent rape, why will she report a date rape where she was drugged in a bar or at a party? I am not a psychologist. I won't try to psychoanalyze the victim. There is another psychological component here. What do we do with the person who administers the drug? He could easily be our co-worker. Does he have the psychological need to administer these date rape drugs to women? That is a problem to be solved by the psychological community.

CHAPTER 4

The main question in this chapter will be answered. The answer may astonish the reader. Many probably feel that trying to rehabilitate a drug addict, alcoholic, or person suffering some type of mental problem is a waste of time. They may feel that there are plenty of other, qualified, clean and sober people deserving a job. That is not always the case. This chapter will show that business is better off helping than replacing. Again, there is plenty for the person needing research. We will see who drinks and who takes drugs. We will see the numbers by age, employment status and industry. Again, this is not a complete study. That would take hundreds of pages and charts. The person in need of the research will get a vivid picture and direction as to where more data can be found.

Just offering the help may not be enough. We will see the various ways in which we get the substance abuser to the EAP or MAP. Some may be obvious and some may shock you. Remember, we are dealing with people who suffer from a disease that tells them they are all right. We will also look back through history to see the attempts to stop people from drinking alcohol. We know, by hindsight, forcing people to abandon cultural traditions and religious rites involving alcohol doesn't work. Trying to force people to refrain from addiction never entered into the picture. Alcoholism and addiction have only recently been recognized as a disease.

Why should management and or unions adopt policies and principles leading toward the treatment substance abuse and mental health?

There were previous attempts to address the problems of alcohol. The Egyptians warned against taverns and excessive drinking. Around 1116 BC, the Chinese issued an edict saying that heaven prescribed moderation with alcohol. As far back as 650 BC it was believed the people would not do without beer and that total abstinence was beyond control of the sages of that era. The Greeks drank moderately. Apparently, there were rules of the day stressing moderate drinking. On to Rome. Was the talk praising Cato the Elder and Caesar for moderation in drinking a subtle hint at the excesses of the time? During the period of Early Christianity, several sects were already calling for abstinence, rejecting wine which was used by Christ as part of the Last Supper and the First Public Miracle, the changing of water into wine at Canna. Warnings against drunkenness are numerous throughout history. Religions and religious leaders while championing the use of wine in their ceremonies warned of the excesses and abuses of alcohol. Drunkenness became a sin. Some religions warned that if you couldn't refrain from abusing alcohol, abstinence was the way to go (Hanson, 2005).

Given the background of the problems caused by chemical dependency in the work place and the fact that is accepted or condoned in many instances, what better place to try and fix the problem than where poses such a great difficulties, the workplace.

In order to answer this question, a great deal of investigation was required. I was very interested in substance abuse, not only among the employed, but the unemployed as well. The reason for my interest is quite simple as will be indicated by reading on. Part of my supporting EAPs and MAPs lie in the problems of replacing qualified employees. I wrote earlier that I wanted to try and place as much information in one place as possible, given the topic. Figures regarding alcoholics and drug addicts have previously been posted in this work. They include those who are working, those who are unemployed, and the potential work force of the future.

This is a very interesting question. Why, indeed, would a company or industry pay good money to help salvage the job of an employee who is causing them to lose money? What are the alternatives to putting assistance programs in place? Wouldn't unions offering assistance to those members suffering from substance abuse be viewed as condoning wrongdoing? Keep in mind that being of legal drinking age and possessing alcohol is not a crime, in itself. Possessing illegal drugs is a crime. Why would unions get involved?

Choices: To treat or not to treat.

There are four obvious choices available to employers and union alike. One is to totally do away with health care benefits. The other is to fire any substance abusing employee or employees who have some other problem that may cause a problem at the job. After dismissing the offender, it will probably become necessary to replace that person. The third obvious choice is to do nothing. The fourth is to keep benefits but see that they change with the times. Neither of the first two options appears to have much appeal.

Do away with all benefits.

Workers have become used to health care benefits. Companies attract qualified people not by salary alone. Chance for advancement and benefits are quite often motivating factors that will induce a prospective employee to choose his or her place of employment. Health care benefits are a valuable bargaining chip in the bidding for quality employees. One of the more alluring aspects of a career in Civil Service is the benefits, both medical and retirement. Benefit packages have become very important to unions. Much time and effort is spent at bargaining tables in the name of benefits.

Fire substance abusing and troubled employees.

Unions and other organizations that protect the interests of the worker do not find that mass firing is acceptable. The firing of substance abusing employees does not appear to make sense, in the light of the available replacement market. There are over 10.5 million alcoholics in the workplace. There are another 10.1 million users of illicit drugs in the workplace. It is not easy to replace that many workers. Many of the afflicted workers have a great deal of skills and knowledge about their particular fields. It could take years to bring a new employee up to the skill level of a person removed from the payroll for chemical dependency. Earlier in this study, figures supporting the rehabilitation of employees were cited. They showed that it serves the general good of the employer to reinvest in the employee. If an employer decided to dismiss all substance abusing employees and replace them, where would he get the replacements? We have already seen the increase in alcohol use and abuse over the past ten years. We have already seen the emergence of new drugs sued by younger people, those who may have just entered or about to enter the workforce. Even more alarming is the fact that many of the evaluation guide lines, those surveys tracking the use and abuse of substances across the board, are using twelve (12) year old, pre teens as base line.

Replacement.

One approach for managers is to get rid of all male abusers and replace them with women. Given the available statistics, that may not be such a good idea. The Center for Substance Abuse and Mental Health Services Administration (SAMHSA), issued a report in 1994 under the title Practical Approaches in the Treatment of Women Who Abuse Alcohol and Other Drugs. The report cites the U.S. Department of Health and Human Services 1990 "Seventh Special Report to the U.S. Congress on Alcohol and Health." The estimated population of women over the age of 12 in 1992 was 107 million. Given that figure it is estimated that women who abuse alcohol is 10.7 million. Excluding the younger teens we find that 6.5% of women between the ages of 18 and 25 admit to heavy alcohol use. Heavy alcohol use or heavy drinking is usually categorized as having 5 or more drinks per occasion in 5 of the past 30 days. The National Household Survey on Drug Abuse conducted a survey in 1991 on the use of alcohol and other drugs. Despite the low number of respondents reporting on polydrug uses, 5.3%, it is important to note that women between 18 and 25 years of age reported using a combination of drugs at the rate of 13.9% (SAMHSA, 1994, pp. 14 & 21). By 1995 the population of women over the age of 12 was estimated in excess of 130 million. Approximately 10 million women aged 18 and over admitted to the use of illicit drugs. Over 65 million women in that age group used alcohol (SAMHSA, 1996, pp. 17 & 83). Another study, though the figures are not quite as devastating, show the chemical dependency problems of today's' woman. A two year study was conducted by the National Center on Addiction and Substance Abuse at Columbia University. This study revealed 4.5 million women are alcoholics or alcohol abusers. The report goes on to say 3.5 million women misuse prescription drugs while an additional 3.1 million report illicit drug use (Bahls, 1998, p., 84).

Looking at women already in the workplace we can disclose figures that may also cause management to see that replacement across the board is not a viable alternative. There is already a problem of alcoholism and illicit drug by women in the workplace. According to the SAMHSA Drug Use Among U.S. Workers (1996) between 1991 and 1993, the years covered by the study, there are approximately 2.1 million accountants, auditors, underwriters, actuaries and bookkeepers. 68.5% are female. Of that number, 3.7% admitted to using illicit drugs while 1.6% admitted to heavy alcohol use. There is the smallest of fractions, .3%, differentiating the males from the women. 4% of men admitted to illicit drug use. Regarding the use of illicit drugs in the past year, 10.1% of the women admit usage while the male population admits to 8.6%. Again, a small difference of only 1.5%. There was a much larger admission regarding heavy alcohol use by men.

Women account for 26% of more that 6 million persons employed in the fields of transportation, communications and public utilities. The women admit to 5.2% currently using illicit drugs. 13.5% admit to the use of illicit drugs in the past year. Again, their percentages are very close to the percentages of men in the same category. There is a large disparity of admission of heavy alcohol use with the use being much higher with males. Women make up approximately 400,000 of the 5,304,081 million construction workers. 11.5% of these women admit to the current use of illicit drugs compared to 12.2% of the men who admitted to current drug use. 13.6% of the women admitted to using illegal drugs within the past year while 21.2% of the men made the same admission. Men admitted to the heavy use of alcohol at 14% while women admitted at 5.2% (Drug Use Among U.S. Workers, 1996, pp. 34, 43, 51, 75, 82, & 83). In light of this information, the author of this study felt that the replacing of chemically abusing men with women was not a viable alternative. Conversely, replacing chemically abusing women with men does not seem to be a solution.

Management may feel that replacing addicted or substance abusing workers with new employees is a viable alternative. This, given the information, may not truly be a wise alternative. In another report, drug and alcohol use among the unemployed was measured. Of the 209 million persons represented in the study, 176 million admitted to the use of alcohol sometime in their life. Of that 176 million, 13.7% of those aged 18 to 25, who are unemployed, admit to heavy alcohol use in the past month. Of those aged 26 to 34, in the same employment category, 9.2% admit to heavy alcohol use in that same time period. For those over 35 years of age the percentage of heavy use of alcohol was 9.9%. This breaks out to almost 11% of the unemployed 18 years of age and older. Those in the same age and employment situations were using marijuana at the rate of 10.8% in the past month. In the previous year, unemployed persons 18 years of age and over used cocaine at the rate of 7.7% while crack use in the same age group for the same time period was almost 4% (SAMHSA, 1996, pp. 89, 100, 45, 57, & 63). Replacing substance abusing workers with unemployed persons appears to have the same value as replacing substance abusing workers of one gender with their opposite gender.

There is no true indication that things will get better in the near future. Heroin use among those aged 18 to 25 in 1995 is as high as it was in the height of the heroin problem of the late 1960s and early 1970s. In 1995 there was a reported increase of 141,000 new heroin users. There was little difference in age groupings. Those 12 to 17 year old first time users were almost equal to new users in the 18 to 25 age group. This marks the largest increase in first time users since data was first collected in 1969. First time use of marijuana among the 12 to 17 year olds' is at an all time high. Those 18 to 25 first time users have dropped since 1994 but the number is still significant. 1980 saw almost 60% of first time users in the 18 to 25 category. The latest report shows that group at 47.7%. This represents the second highest percentage of first time users in that age group since 1980. First time use of hallucinogens is at an all time high. Both age groups show significant increases in first time users. There are increases in first time users of both alcohol, and cocaine in both age groups. From 1991 to 1994 first time cocaine use by those 18 to 25 dropped. However, the increase in 1995 is 3%. The 12 to 17 group also rose approximately 3%. Their percentage was their highest in over a decade representing the second highest increase in first time users since the onset of keeping such records in 1963 (Preliminary Results from the 1996 Household Survey on Drug Abuse, 1997, pp. 102, 98, 101, 103, & 99). Putting industry on hold and waiting of the next generation of workers does not make much sense, in light of the available data regarding the youth of today. The rate of the use of illicit drugs by all young people from 12 to 17 years of age has risen substantially since 1992. Children who use illicit drugs, alcohol, and tobacco, increase their chances for life time dependency. The average age for a child first using alcohol has declined. They are drinking at a younger age (National Drug control Strategy, 1997).

Do Nothing.

The option of doing nothing is not a pragmatic solution. This information contained here shows the cost of chemical dependency to business. To take a do-nothing approach will not serve any purpose other than increasing the loss of company revenue.

The issue of the necessity and value of employee and member assistance programs becomes real. We will soon see many case studies where the value and efficacy of assistance programs are shown. We have already seen the need for them. Those studies indicate a solid reason for assistance programs. The bottom line benefits in a positive mode. Companies have a better, more productive employee. Unions have a healthier member who positively impacts the union bottom line. That person continues on as an active dues payer. The union member may quite possibly present the added value of a peer counselor, a valuable component of union based assistance programs.

The only way the success or failure of any program can be measured is if people choose to avail themselves of that program. The use of workplace assistance programs is no different. This leads to how do people access the programs that are available to them? Before we can access as assistance program, we should know what they are.

There are three basic assistance programs that are concerned with assisting employees and union members. One is an Employee Assistance Program (EAP). This is a program administered by management that deals with workplace problems of chemical dependency, mental health, and other issues that affect the performance of an employee.

> An employee assistance program (EAP) is a worksite-based program designed to assist in the identification and resolution of productivity problems associated with employees impaired by personal concerns including, but not limited to: health, marital, family, financial, alcohol, drug, legal, emotional, stress, or other personal concerns which may adversely affect employee job performance (Scanlon, 1991, p. 103).

The second is a Member Assistance Program (MAP). It is a program similar to an EAP but administered and managed by a union or other organizations that represent an employee.

In contrast to EAPs, which tend to emphasize the roles of supervisors and clinicians in helping troubled workers get treatment, MAPs emphasize the role of peer counselors-union members who volunteer their time to prevent substance abuse and help their co-workers who have substance abuse problems. MAPs are built around the idea of union members helping one another stay sober and "clean" (i.e., drug-free). This is not a new idea. It is the basis of the craft unionism, and the existence of labor-based programs for assisting members is as old as the labor movement itself (Bacharach, Bamberger & Sonnenstuhl, 1994, p 5).

Looking at the descriptions of the first two programs we see a commonality. EAPs refer to the employee while MAPs refer to the member. Both employee and member could be one and the same person. Another common point is the choice of words regarding abuse or addiction. The employee programs refer to drugs, alcohol, and stress. The member programs refer to alcohol in the use of the word "sober" and the word drugs.

The third type of program is a Joint Union/Management Program, a program for assisting an employee jointly administered and managed by both management and unions. However, the move toward jointly run and administered programs was not as easy as it appears.

The EAP concept is hollow unless labor is a willing participant. Although organized labor and management generally cooperate on common goals today, it was not always so. Historically, labor-management antagonism often fostered concerns that EAPs would never be established.... Hindsight aside, it should be remembered that organized labor and management reached their present reasonably friendly and cooperative relationship only after considerable trial and travail marked by mutual fear and mistrust. Some of these once-characteristic feelings occasionally found their way into early efforts to organize programs to assist troubled workers (Bickerton, 1990, p. 38).

Whatever the chief motivating factor for program implementation, there is one constant: People. The union agenda may differ from the management agenda but the reality is that people are at the core of the problem as well as the solution. Unions and management can work together to help the problem faced by their members and the employees. An examination of the programs shows a great deal of similarity. Before a joint program could be introduced, the issue of trust had to be addressed.

> ...The EAP is frequently seen as a device of the personnel department for the purpose of reducing costs and/ or facilitating compliance with progressive disciplinary action procedures. This is true even when the program is a function of the organizations' medical department. Consequently, the management EAP is likely to be used by unions only as a last resort to circumvent disciplinary action against union members. This is not to say that all management programs are eschewed by union members, but establishing any level of trust may take years to achieve (Scanlon, 1991, pp. 118-119).

Looking at the history of unions in helping the membership by offering help with many problems, there does not appear to be a significant difference between the two programs. Unions have had a broad brush approach to assistance for much of their history. Management programs are also not limited to the area of chemical dependency. With both opposing camps offering the same type of help it appears that they should be working together. One benefit of a joint program is that the employee will know of its existence. There should be a buy-in by the union. Another benefit to the union is one of costs. Quite often the company will pick up the cost of running such a program.

> Once a management-sponsored EAP is established, it is not likely to be later developed into a true labor-management program. Unless the union is invited to participate in the development of policies, procedures, and program implementation at the onset, the EAP still be viewed as a

management program with all of its limitations (Scanlon, 1991, p. 119).

The principal component to the joint program is trust and if management wants the union to trust in the program, the union must be in from the beginning. The conflicting ideology of both parties can be put aside if both parties are involved in the program from the beginning, even if management is paying for the program. This cooperative effort should lead to a more effective program and prove more cost effective (Scalnon, 1991).

All assistance programs are not called EAP or MAP or Join Assistance Programs. some go by other names. Trans World Airlines call their program Special Health Services. Metropolitan Life Insurance Company calls their program Employee Advisory Services. Some unions alter the program name and call it a Union Assistance Program. Whatever the name, the reason for their existence remains the same. They handle the problems of working people and their families.

Regardless of the type of assistance program, they will never be successful unless people avail themselves of their services. In other words, employees or members must gain access to the programs.

Accessing an EAP or MAP.

Assistance access is not relegated solely to the work site. Employees can access assistance through methods and avenues such as the criminal justice system. That could be resultant of an arrest for a violation involving drugs or alcohol or a result of an incident of domestic violence. It is possible that an employed individual might be referred to an assistance program by a child care advocacy agency. In keeping with the main theme of this work, the work place and problems caused by chemical dependency problems and mental health issues, three main avenues of access were addressed. Those avenues were self-referral, managerial referral and union referral or peer pressure. A component that could be integrated into the realm of managerial referrals might be a referral by the company medical department.

Self Referral.

In attending Alcoholics Anonymous meetings one may hear a phrase that is very familiar to AA; "I'm sick and tired of being sick and tired." A phrase as innocently sounding as this could be a reason for a person seeking treatment or assistance as a self referral. A self recognized decline in production or life style might be the catalyst challenging an individual to seek assistance through a program. Family pressure or health problems may cause help seeking. The previously mentioned violation of law may not end with a judge's recommendation to seek help. Still, the individual may see that the predicament at hand was caused by chemical abuse. That incident may be the issue that allows an individual to seek help through the various available assistance programs.

In an organization with a comprehensive program capable of handling problems in a broad brush fashion, the rate of self referral is apt to be considerably higher than a program that focuses solely on chemical dependency. The broad brush program is one that does not limit itself to issues of substance abuse. It covers all manner of problems that may cause problems for the employee or member. Employees with problems such as gambling, needing some type of social service, having relationship difficulties and other problems are more likely to seek help for those matters than for chemical dependency. For the most part a person with marital problems, for example, is in denial and does not see the problem possibly being related to chemical dependency. The individual may blame the increase in chemical usage on the marital problem, seeing the use of drugs and or alcohol as a problem solution (Scanlon, 1991, p. 78).

Managerial referral.

No matter how poorly things may go for an employed alcoholic or drug addict outside the work site, many manage to remain in the ranks of the employed. As long as the pay check keeps coming in the individual may justify abusing chemicals. The individual can feel that all is not so bad. He or she is working and providing. This places the management in a unique position. They, the management, are the people who are more likely to recognize the problem than the problem person. They are in a position to do something about the individual and the problem.

> The employer is in a unique position to exert some pressure on the alcoholic at a relatively early stage. Recommending that he go for treatment may well be a precipitating factor in a recovery. The fact that the boss sees the problems and calls a spade a spade can go far in breaking down the denial system. Keeping his job may be important enough to get the alcoholic to begin to see his problem more realistically (Kinney & Leaton, 1978, p. 125).

This type of action by a manager could be viewed as an intervention, a method of getting the employee motivated enough to seek help for the problem. Although not often the case, it is best to have an intervention at the earliest manifestation of problems.

> Early intervention benefits from a focus on what people do right, without belaboring what they do wrong. We also need to eliminate other barriers to behavior changed. One of the biggest barriers is the stigma attached to addictive disorders. There is a tremendous stigma attached to someone being called an 'alcoholic, "drug addict," or "mentally ill." It is interesting that people are often willing to accept a mental illness tag before they are willing to accept an addiction diagnosis (McClellan, 1990, p. 76).

It is not enough that a supervisor or manager be empowered to refer an employee to the employee assistance program. The supervisor should know how to identify a potential or existing problem. They should also have knowledge of the five, generally accepted, methods for dealing with problems. They are recognition, documentation, action, referral, and reintegration.

If a problem exists regarding the deterioration of work performance, the manager must recognize that issue before it can be placed before the individual. This recognition can be as simple as smelling alcohol on the breath of an employee in the morning or after returning from lunch. The keys are recognition, not diagnosis and observation, not evaluation.

Without proper documentation of managerial observances, a well meaning intervention might turn into a confrontation. A "my word against your word" argument may begin. Quite possibly, the employee is unaware of the deterioration of performance. In that case the manager or supervisor should be able to present a documentation of dwindling performance.

If action in the form of discipline, such as suspension or a warning, is to take place, it is important that the action be consistent with the disciplinary policies of the organization.

When a referral is made to the program, it is important that a description of the behavior be forwarded. This could be an invaluable tool that will enable the counselor to penetrate the defense of denial. Denial of chemical dependency is quite prevalent. Dependent persons deny their abuse and often their denial is supported by family and friends. People may defend a dependent person by saying things like, "Joe drinks a little too much on occasion but he isn't an alcoholic. He goes to work everyday," or "Mary does a few lines of coke on the weekends but she does not have a problem." Earlier, I touched on people not believing they have a problem. The paycheck helps to bolster the feeling that all is fine. There is no problem. The information forwarded to the program personnel may help the counselor in formulating an action or treatment plan. The information documented in the report sent to the counselor takes on a high degree of significance in reducing denial (McClellan, 1990). McClellan (1990) said that people would rather have the reputation associated with a mental health problem than be known as an addicted person.

It is important that management know how to deal with the problems of chemical dependence in the work place. Managers may need training in working with employees in this venue. Failure to train properly will probably lead to failure of a program. Unless a supervisor is trained in how to properly conduct an intervention, it may turn into a confrontation. Supervisors should make sure that they are acting on their own observations and not on rumor, gossip or off the job behavior. Lack of preparation may impede the process of having the employee access the help needed to have the employee return to normal functioning.

> If a lack of such supervisory skills is organization-wide, then the EAP will fail. In order to prevent this failure, supervisors must learn the techniques and the process. Rather than firing or transferring troubled employees to other departments to "get rid" of the problem, the EAP deals with the problem in a direct manner, reducing chemical dependency throughout the organization (Scanlon, 1991, p. 45).

Another type of managerial referral may come through the company medical department. The doctor may recognize symptoms that are related to alcohol abuse or drug abuse. Cocaine use can cause sleeplessness and weight loss along with erratic mood changes or swings. Alcohol abuse may be indicated by liver problems. Scanlon (1991) calls this type of referral a "soft referral."

Union referral or peer pressure.

For well over one hundred years unions and peers have been in the forefront of the fight against alcohol in the work place. Bacharach et. al. (1994) made several citations. In the 1830s, the Boston Working Men's Protective Union required their membership, among other things, to refrain from using alcohol (Staudenmeier, 1985). Another citation referred to the Washingtonians, a prototype of AA. This organization was formed by six individuals. Their goal was to save workers from drunkenness and keep them sober (Blumberg, 1991). Temperance relying on self-help and mutual aid in assisting members with drinking problems was encouraged by the Knights of Labor and the National Labor Union. Other labor organization recognizing the need for helping their fellows formed temperance focused self-help groups. The Sons of Temperance, the Good Templars, and the Red, White, and Blue Clubs were such organizations (Ames, Fall 1989, p. 495; Bacharach et al, 1994, p. 10).

Earlier I offered information in regards to assistance programs popping up in the World War Two years. Since that time organized labor has been promoting the further development of EAP and MAP programs. Today, there is the National Council on Alcoholism and Drug Dependence, formerly called the National Council on Alcoholism and the Employees Assistance Professionals Association (EAPA). This organization was previously known as the Association of Labor-Management Administrators and Consultants on Alcoholism (ALMACA) (Bacharach, et al, 1994, p. 10-11). Another organization of unionists heavily involved in the assistance program arena is the Labor Assistance Professionals (LAP). The Employee Assistance Professionals Association has recently expanded its' board of directors to include a labor chair.

Philosophical differences in breadth and scope of Assistance Programs.

A problem surrounding the issue of joint programs may lie in the different philosophies. Management programs seem to embrace the broad brush concept of assistance. Unions are divided along those lines. Some unions want to remain traditional in the assistance field. This flies in the face of their past where they provided a myriad of services to their members. They want to limit themselves to substance abuse alone. Bickerton (1990) reports that Leo Perlis was not a champion of broad brush programs. Perlis believed that a broad brush approach was diversionary and was not as scientific as a contemporary union program dealing strictly with alcohol. He may have been in fear of assistance programs losing focus on the alcohol problems of the workers. He did not want to see alcohol programs become broad brush to the point where they would attempt to cover so many issues that they would not be effective (Bickerton, 1990,

p. 40). On the railroad, Operation:RedBlock is still focusing on chemical dependency. This was not the view of an earlier labor picture regarding assisting their membership. Bamberger & Sonnenstuhl (1995) report several major unions as providers of help other than substance abuse. Their citation indicates the Teamsters, the International Ladies Garment Workers, and the United Mine Workers provided their members with psychiatric services. In the 1940s a variety of mental health services, along with substance abuse services, were made available to union members (Ferguson & Fersing, 1965). Bacharach, et al. (1994) say the flight attendants programs began dealing with substance abuse issues and broadened the scope of the programs to handle more issues, such as mental health.

Broad Brush.

Earlier I reported the findings of Scanlon (1991), wherein the self referral rate was higher in programs that had a broad brush approach. A person with a gambling problem may want to speak with a counselor about his problem. A person having difficulty with a marriage may want to seek counseling for the difficulties. This may be a way to have the problems of chemical dependency brought to the fore.

The study also reported that some people would rather be known as having a mental health problem than a chemical dependency problem. That has changed somewhat over the past decades but is still prevalent in some cultures and segments of society. I didn't totally grasp that concept until I met a recovering man who treated alcoholics, and ran numerous after care groups and interventions. We became quite close friends. His being Jewish brought the claim that "people would rather be known as having a mental problem than a chemical dependency problem" into a more meaningful light when he told me, jokingly, "There is no such thing as a Jewish alcoholic. We all have nervous breakdowns". We know that chemical dependency is an equal opportunity destroyer, having no boundaries on gender, race, religion, or class distinctions. To think, even in joking, there could very well be people choosing to let it be known they have a mental health problem instead of admitting to alcoholism or drug addiction, just added to the magnitude of the problem.

When other issues are addressed, it could be determined that a broad brush approach be adopted by union, management and joint assistance programs.

The broad brush approach affords people the opportunity to seek help for problems not always associated with employee or member assistance programs. Many individuals believe that assistance programs are strictly for handling problems of substance abuse. They do not realize that programs deal with many other issues. The history of union programs, addressed later, shows the past involvement in dealing with problems other than substance abuse.

Coercion.

Another method of getting a person to accept that there is a problem is the use of coercion. This tactic can be used by both union and management. This coercion is psychological and monetary, not physical. No one is going to come to the home of an alcoholic or drug addict, put a bag over the head and carry them away into the night. Treatment will not be physically forced on an individual. Most people know there are choices. The substance abuser has the right to refuse the help offered by a join union-management program or a MAP. In the case of the working person, the desired benefit could be the salary and continued employment. The value of the paycheck can not be overlooked. It is an extremely powerful tool. In 1988, Mark de Bernardo, the director of the Institute for a Drug Free America, felt America was failing in winning the war on drugs. He felt that government, law enforcement, and schools could not win the war alone. He believed that these institutions needed the help of corporate America to win the war. He claimed that employers had the most powerful weapon available in the war, the paycheck. de Bernardo felt the power to withhold the paycheck should be wielded in an effort to keep employees drug free (de Bernardo, 1988). The unemployed can also be coerced into accepting treatment if he or she is faced with the loss of public assistance benefits. A study conducted in Brooklyn, New York by Frances O. Mark, Ph.D., showed that one third of patients referred by a person with the ability to withhold anticipated rewards stayed in treatment. Only one fifth of those completing treatment were from agencies or work based programs that did not have to power of coercion (Mark, 1988, pp. 11-13).

The union-management combination in a joint EAP venture can have a tremendous impact in getting a person into treatment. If a person is represented by a union and that person feels infringed upon, he or she may file a grievance against the manager. Earlier in the study the problem facing managers being grieved by employees for suggesting substance abuse or the need for EAP was discussed. What was not discussed is what happens to the grievant when the management and the union are in some type of agreement regarding a problem. Both parties can approach the issue from their respective areas of familiarization. Management can tell the employee that the behavior surrounding the job performance or absenteeism will not be tolerated. The union can take the position that it can not tolerate the self destruction of one of it members. The member may be looking toward the union to grieve the action by the manager. If the managerial action is appropriate and there is a joint program, when the employee approaches the union, he or she will hear the union saying the same thing about the problem. Hopefully, this approach will help all concerned parties by keeping the issues away from the grievance table. Without a joint program, there is the possibility that infraction regarding assistance issues will be handled in an adversarial arena, the grievance table. Management will probably discipline an employee for violation of rules and policies regarding substance abuse on the job or in the work place. The union will defend the member, even if the member is wrong. If the union wins they will more than likely face the same problem at a later date. The progression of the problem will continue and performance will worsen. It is more than likely that the person will eventually lose the job (Scanlon, 1991, p. 120). If coercion is the ability to withhold an anticipate reward then this joint assistance program is coercive. Management is threatening to withhold the anticipated salary, benefits and future employment. On the other hand the union is saying that agrees with the assessment of management. They may not agree with the discipline taken but they can reaffirm the company position in that unless the person gets help there is little that the union can do. The union can not come out and say that it will withhold services to the member. It can infer that there is a strong need for the individual to get help before they can be successful in the grievance procedure.

There is one particularly dangerous tactic that can be employed in a coercive manner. That is a therapeutic dismissal.

This is where both management and union want to help the employee but the denial is so great, the employee can not see the problem. The union and management union meet and agree that the person be fired, but there are ground rules. The union will tell the employee that the only way they can get him or her reinstated is if the individual agrees to seek help for their particular problem. If that individual gets help, he or she will placed back on the payroll. The most important factor in therapeutic dismissals is a clear cut understanding that if the individual refuses to go for help he or she is still placed back on the payroll. Naturally, the employee has no knowledge of this deal. The individual may see the light. That person may not go into treatment for substance abuse, but he or she might be scared enough to completely stop or greatly reduce the drinking and drugging. I recommend this tactic as an absolute last resort. I also recommend that the possibility of such action be discussed by management and the union person responsible for the MAP. No elected union official will own up to advocating the dismissal of a member, even if a reinstatement deal has been made before the action. That official should not be put in such a position.

The coercive manner is different in the joint union-management program than it is in the MAP regarding work performance. In the joint program, poor performance allows the supervisor the opportunity to intervene. In the negotiations that follow, performance becomes a motivator for employees changing their behavior. The MAP is not hampered by the restraints that impede the joint plan. Management can not and should not react to gossip, rumor or off duty behavior. The MAP can. In the members program, the counselors and peers may confront the worker with rumor, gossip and talk of their off duty habits. Joint assistance plans look at the work performance. The MAP will use evidence garnered from the work place or through the rumor mill. They will not solely focus on problems or unsafe actions at work. They will focus on how drinking or drugging or other negative action is affecting their private lives and the lives of their families (Sonnenstuhl &

Trice, 1987, p. 248). Bacharach, et al (1996) speak about union peer counselors teaming up with co-workers in attempting to break down the denial of a troubled worker. The advice given by the peer counselor is often unsolicited. The employees are approached about behavior. They are confronted with evidence related to the problem and are encouraged to seek help. Often the peer counselor will team up with a supervisor in attempting to break the denial barriers. Bacharach, et al (1994) tell how joint action by supervisors and peer counselors came to be viewed as an explanation for getting troubled workers to go to the MAP in the transportation industry.

Coercion is a valuable weapon in the battle for getting people to seek help. A person may expect an argument from the place of employment regarding the excessive use of alcohol or drugs. That person, if coming from a union represented company will probably not be prepared for a union position agreeing, in substance, with management, that there is a problem with the employee/member. It is important that the focus on choice never be forgotten. Sometime the denial of a problem is so deep, regardless of how well motivated and informed the counselors are, the employee refuses to accept the fact that help is needed.

Unions should not be viewed negatively in regards to coercion. Coercion is but one tactic available to both parties. The MAPs did things other than coerce. The MAPs deterred substance abuse through other methods. They viewed referral and long term follow up as part of a program of deterrence as well as abuse prevention. They were explicit in regards to the union position surrounding the issue of abuse both on and off the job. They acted in the capacity of agents of cultural change. They fought to change the cultural denial of the problem that prevailed on the side of both occupational people and the organizations. They maintain a broad brush approach for assistance and offer a variety of treatment options. They also encourage their members to utilize self-help groups like AA to manage their problems over the long term (Bacharach, et al, 1994, pp. 79-80).

Management has a reason for offering EAPs. It is socially acceptable; it makes them look responsible; it shows that they are observant in watching their employees and the ability to spot problems, and it saves them money. There is nothing wrong with that attitude.

There are many of reasons for unions to help their members and their families as we have seen and will see more as we proceed.

Regardless of the reason for a union-management program the overall consensus is that they work better than a single entity program as long as the interests at the same. Both have to be on the same page at the same time. They work.

R. Brinkley Smithers was not a Union Man. He was a very successful banker, a multi millionaire and a recovering alcoholic. He was a pioneer in studying alcohol in the workplace and is responsible for the Smithers Institute for Alcohol-Related Workplace Studies at Cornell University. He knew that management couldn't get the job done regarding substance abuse in the workplace. Labor had to be involved. He offered this advice to major corporations like General Motors and the steel companies. His support of union management based programs manifested itself in the Seagram Company.

Peer Counseling, examples of successful union programs, and coercion as a tool

A union represented worker may be referred to the MAP through peer counselors. These are usually persons who have experienced the same problems and are in recovery. Recovery is a term used by people who have learned to live life without giving into their addiction. The term recovery is preferred over the term recovered. Recovered has a ring of finality to it. The past tense indicates that it has already happened. Chemical dependency clients are taught that the sobriety or remaining drug free is a never ending process. Peers act as an example that the programs work. There is life without drinking and drugging. Peer counseling is often initiated by a co-worker who is in the Alcoholics Anonymous fellowship.

<u>Sandhogs.</u>

One of the successful uses of peers is indicated in the program involving the sandhogs. For some time, labor and management have been at odds over work place drinking. This issue has been fought in hearings taking place before arbitrators. For the most part the arbitrators have ruled that management cannot discipline workers for drinking unless their work performance is adversely affected. This policy could be viewed as leading to the drinking of the sandhogs. Recall that there are no managers in the hole. The foremen and walking bosses are all union members. If the worker was adversely affected by alcohol or drug use, the only one who would know of the problem is the co-worker, the equal on the job, the peer. Sonnenstuhl and Trice (1987) cite Winick in his description of peer counseling programs as generally assisting members and their families in areas of marital and financial difficulty, legal and other problems. Peer counseling is not just a program dealing with chemical dependency (Winick, 1985).

At the time of their study of the sandhog MAP Sonnenstuhl and Trice (1987) noted that there were two full time counselors. These counselors were credentialed alcoholism counselors, having attended The Rutgers Summer School of Alcohol Studies. They also attended the one year alcohol training program as South Oaks Hospital. South Oaks has the reputation of being a prestigious institution located on Long Island, NY. Along with these study programs, the counselors attended numerous work shops and conferences on alcoholism. Both these men were members of AA and had many years experience of doing Twelfth Step work. The Twelfth Step is one of the steps recommended by AA that will help maintain sobriety. The Twelfth Step suggests that a recovering person go and help another individual who needs help in getting sober or remaining drug free. This lets the person know that he or she is not alone. In keeping with the Twelfth Step, the Peer Counselors utilize a network of recovering alcoholics and drug addicts to help get the word to others who may need help. These counselors also received training in peer counseling from the New York City Central Labor Council. One thing that sets these counselors apart from a management program is that when they were not at the work site networking with members who were having problems, they were taking members to AA meetings.

We have seen management embrace programs for their own reasons. So did the sandhog union. The union funded the programs with money from their welfare fund. The union also encouraged contractors to voluntarily contribute to the fund. The union faced some serious problems given the unique position of no management working. They diverted from a typical industry standard of placing an individual in jeopardy of losing the job. Since union members could not lose their place on a gang for job performance, they could not be expelled from the union. The counselors had difficulty in speaking with members about possibly losing their job if they failed to control or curtail their drinking. They also faced the dilemma that if they did nothing, the member may die. One sandhog dies for every mile of tunnel dug.

As recently as 1970, the sandhogs had approximately six members belonging to A.A. Today, as estimated by the sandhog union, 11% of the membership has been sober for one year or more (Sonnenstuhl & Trice, 1987, pp. 225-227 & 235). This not an indication that the other 89% are alcoholics. The study reports on sandhogs in AA. In looking back at drinking in the construction trades, we recall that 14% of the men admitted to heavy use of alcohol. That may be an indication of alcoholism. Some may get control of the drinking. The 11% sober as reported by the sandhogs appears to be validation of the success of their own program.

Two other successful examples of MAPs lie in the airline and railroad industries. These industries have their own employee assistance programs, but the unions maintain separate programs. Their success lies in the support for the programs from the membership as well as the union leadership. Management, on the other hand, was cost conscious. They utilized agencies that claimed the provision of services similar to on site employee assistance programs. Too often these services were no more than counselor staffed telephone lines. The MAPs were different. They used a network of peer counselors at the work site whether it was moving or stationary. The union peer counselors had a great deal of autonomy. This afforded them entrance into the sub-cultural world and social network of those in need of assistance. They were not management. They could gain the trust of the people (Bacharach, et al, pp. 34-35).

AFA EAP.

The Association of Flight Attendants (AFA) represents some 30,000 members employed by 18 carriers. Their initial support came by way of a grant from the National Institute of Alcohol Abuse and Alcoholism (NIAAA). This was to be a joint program. The carriers intervened and the program never got off the ground. The carriers wanted the AFA program to include all airline employees and demanded that the AFA take a limited role in the referral process. The AFA refused. The carriers developed an EAP that served all airline employees. When the NIAAA funding period came to an end, the AFA EAP started their own assistance program with the union assuming the full financial burden of the program.

> The goal of the AFA EAP is to help flight attendants deal with a wide range of personal problems, including chemical dependency.... Much of the success of the program is due to the network of active flight attendants who volunteer their time and energy to act as peer counselors. None of these counselors are paid for EAP work, and they do it all in addition to their regular jobs. Depending on case loads and circumstances, the counselors may spend considerable time working for the EAP (Bacharach et al, 1994, p., 17).

The counselors are trained at AFA headquarters. They are trained in handling in acting as both passive and active counselors. They are also trained in crisis handling. The counselors seek out their troubled co-workers and provide unsolicited recommendations that are relative to their behavior. Observations by co-workers, other employees, and management can prompt a peer counselor to take action. At each home base the peer counselors form a committee. This committee works with other committees such as grievance, health and safety, and committees responsible for professional standards (Bacharach et al, 1994, pp., 16 & 17).

Railroad EAP.

Knowing the culture and their peers enabled the MAP of the railroad workers to assist in addressing a problem faced by the railroad of over 100 years. The study previously showed the failure of management instituted Rules G and E. The concerns of management continued. They were worried that people would select alternate modes of travel and freight shippers would find other methods of shipping their goods. A railroad brakeman, Jimmy Dargon of the Union Pacific Railroad came up with a new approach, a by-pass of Rule G. This concept is called Operation:RedBlock. An employee of the railroad in violation of Rule G could seek assistance without penalty of dismissal. Managers could refer a violator of Rule G to the EAP for treatment. The employee would have to comply with the counselor. Red Block had a "marking off" system helping to keep workers who have been drinking or drugging off the job, without penalty. A worker who had been drinking or taking drugs and was called to work could mark him or herself off. This is treated as an excused absence. If a person reports to work as scheduled and who is also by affected by drugs or alcohol, that person may also mark off. If a worker is impaired and does not mark off, a co-worker can mark the person off and send that person home. After being marked off, the RedBlock committee, a group comprised of union members speaks with the offender. A determination is then made as to what will transpire. Despite being a relatively new program, RedBlock seems to be successful although the railroads using this program are few in numbers. Two companies reporting success are Amtrak and CSX Transportation (Bacharach, et al, 1994, pp. 20-21). Here, again, we see leverage at work but not necessarily from management. The union is putting pressure on the member.

<u>Summary.</u>

We have seen why corporations and unions should provide help to their employees. There are not only traditions that need to be upheld, there are economic reasons. One glaring similarity is the issue of job performance. Some would have us believe that job performance is not a concern of Union Assistance Programs or Union Assistance Counselors. Nothing could be further from the truth. Self referrals, as we have seen, often see their own personal decline in the workplace and identify the fact that they may have a problem and actively seek help. Managers are often the first to observe a worker declining in productivity and attendance. In Union Shops, the steward is quite often the first to recognize the same decline the management has noticed. Previously we have seen that management is often reluctant to approach a worker who may have a problem. A properly trained steward knows how to reach out. We know that the job is often the catalyst for seeking assistance. Helping a worker recognize that dependence on alcohol, drugs, or other matters that are negatively impacting on his or her productivity and attendance is all that might be needed to direct that individual to seek help. The steward co-worker is an invaluable tool. Who better to recognize a problem than the person who shares the similar work experience, same conditions, same management, a like amount of service time, a person you eat with, and maybe ally with in office or shop sports team, a union brother or sister?

The data supports the excessive risk involved in dismissing offenders and replacing them with those from the ranks of the unemployed. There are no clear cut indicators that these problems will improve. In the arenas where unions are involved we have seen where they can do things management can not. They can refer to the rumor mill and activity of the member outside the workplace. We also see where it would be difficult for management to do away with the benefits long and hard bargained for by the unions. We have seen the benefit of union and management working together in a jointly run program.

The philosophical differences and approaches by both management and unions were discussed. The one thing they have in common is they deal with people. There are differences. These differences are not necessarily bad. We just can not have one group dictating policy. When looking at the AFA program, we see the need for a separate program. The philosophical differences were too broad. Both management and union wanted to use the broad brush approach but management wanted the union to take a limited role in the area of referral to treatment. The airline management also wanted the union program to handle the problems of all employees, not just flight attendants. The union started the program and eventually funded it, without management support. On the railroad, the programs was started to primarily handle the problem of alcohol abuse. The benefits of a broad brush approach when compared to one of dealing with substance abuse problems, only shows the ability to help more people. Just because a person does not have a substance abuse problem, that does not mean he or she is not in need of as services available under assistance programs. A broad brush approach could easily lead on to see that they do have a substance abuse problem that leads to other problems. The reverse could also be true. Personal problems that go unattended could lead to substance abuse issues.

A good deal of emphasis has been placed on the use of leverage or coercion. The value of coercion can not be underestimated. It should be handled with a great deal of care. One must be careful that ulterior motives on behalf of either management or unions not come to the fore. Coercion should be an asset. One must be wary that it does not become a vindictive tool.

CHAPTER 5

When I first started to gather information, I found the information to be spread all over the place. There really isn't one spot where this data is readily available in volume. It took time to compile all the case studies showing that EAPs, MAPs, and rehabilitating the employee/member is worth the time and effort. The case studies go from the 70s to the present time. If you are not interested in this type of data you may want to skip this chapter. It contains successful studies and a relatively few unsuccessful studies. In my search for positive results I naturally found some negatives but not many. However, if you want to read about successful programs in well known, multi-national companies and some smaller companies, here it is. I hope this serves the needs of those who require research.

Do Assistance Programs work to reduce absenteeism, on-the-job accidents, and employee turnover, due to employee substance abuse problems?

Earlier, we examined the negative impact chemical dependency has on and in the workplace. The problem needed to be addressed. The questions regarding assistance program become what type of approach or approaches to the problem works and are they worth the effort? Different industries combined with different locations and employee bases may require diverse programs. In all probability a "one size fits all" EAP/MAP is not appropriate. The problem of substance abuse and mental health affect a multitude of work environs, not just one industry in one location. The question is one of great importance to both employers and employees. It is a question of monetary value. The bottom line needs to be looked at. Is helping the employee worth the effort and cost?

Baltimore Union/Management study results.

A study of employee programs was conducted in Baltimore, MD. in 1972. The study found that the programs were, indeed, cost-effective. The study involved both unions and management in a dozen companies that employed 134,000 persons, collectively. That study showed that the cost for 206 patients referred to treatment was $230.000. This translated into the combined employers saving of $454,000 in the first year. The second year showed a greater improvement to $600,000 saved through increased attendance at work. The following year the savings were predicted to be $1 million with savings expected to grow geometrically each year thereafter. The areas in which improvements were indicated were in decreased absenteeism, and reduction in on-the-job accidents. Morale improved leading to an increase in production. Less equipment damaged was also noted (Kinney & Leaton, 1978, pp. 257-258).

General Motors of Canada Limited.

On July 1, 1976, an unpublished report on the GM Canadian Alcoholism Recovery Program and was released as a personal communication. It compared results of those alcoholics participating in the program against a control group of non-participants. The control group was classified as persons not undergoing treatment despite the indication of a need for a program. Program participants consisted of 104 employees undergoing active treatment for alcoholism. The non-program participants numbered 48 employees. Alcoholic participants showed a 48% decrease in sickness and accident claims. There was a 48% decrease in the number of days lost and a 48% decrease in the amount paid for sickness and accidents. There was a 27% decrease in workers' compensation claims and an 84% decrease in the number of lost days under the provisions provided for under workers' compensation. A decrease in of amounts paid in workers' compensation benefits was 64%. The 48 non-participating alcoholic employees showed an increase of 48% in the number of sickness and accident claims and a 121% increase in the number of days lost. There was an increase of 128% in the amount paid for sickness and disability benefits. There was an increase of 25% in workers' compensation benefit claims and a 77% increase in the number of days lost under the provisions provided by workers' compensation. There was an increase of 77% in the amount paid in workers' compensation benefits (Pontius, p., 18).

<u>United States Navy.</u>

On July 1, 1977, a summary of a cost benefit study was prepared for the Chief of Navy Personal, Navy Alcohol Prevention Personnel, in Washington, DC. The study was reported to be one of the most extensive in the area of cost effectiveness. The rigorous criteria were used in studying over 5,000 Navy and US Marine Corps personnel. This study showed it was cost effective regarding the retention of personnel. The Department of Navy spent $22.6 million for the rehabilitation of alcoholics. They calculated that it would cost the Navy $49 million to achieve the same number of years of future service if these persons were replaced.

The success rate showed remarkable differences. The effectiveness of the treatment varied by almost 40% in two significant age groups. That part of the population, over the age of 26 years, was viewed as essentially career personnel. Treatment effectiveness for this age group was 83%. Those under the age of 25 years and who had undergone alcohol rehabilitation had a 44% rate of success. These figures were based on a two year post treatment evaluation. Regarding absenteeism prior to treatment, alcoholics were absent three times, 8.1 days annually, more often than the average service member of the Navy and the Marine Corps. After successful rehabilitation their rate of absenteeism returned the sick day average to 2.7 days per person, per year. There was also a large overall large cost savings through the reduction of the demands of health care services amounting to $5.5 million with an additional savings of $2.3 million in the area of outpatient health care (Pontius, p., 18).

The Department of the Navy, while appearing to be somewhat tolerant of alcoholics, was not as tolerant as some companies in the private sector. Self insured unions would allow several attempts at rehabilitation. AT&T and NYNEX both allowed more that one rehabilitation. The Navy allowed only one. In a question and answer session with representatives with then President Regan's Committee for a Drug Free

America (1988), the author of this study inquired about the Navy and its position on repeated attempts at rehabilitation. The response was the Navy allowed one attempt at rehabilitation. If there was a relapse, they would put that person through another rehabilitation but upon release from the rehabilitation facility, that person would be discharged from the military.

Kennecott Copper Corporation.

In 1978, the Kennecott Copper Corporation performed two studies. One study was conducted with 37 alcoholics, 18 of whom chose not to participate. Twelve individuals were referred to the INSIGHT Program. Absenteeism was reduced by 49.5%. Weekly indemnity was improved by 64.2%. Hospital, medical, and surgical costs were reduced by 48.9%. The 2% not involved in the INSIGHT Program showed an increase in absenteeism by 2.9%, an increase in weekly indemnity of 28.5%, and an increase in hospital, medical, and surgical costs of 7.4%. The second study involved 83 employees and the INSIGHT Program. Before program participation the absenteeism average rate for the group was 3.81 days over 11.5 months. After INSIGHT, absenteeism decreased by 44% in 64 persons and increased by 37.2% in the remaining 18 persons.

In May 1981, a follow up survey of the INSIGHT Program at Kennecott was conducted. Eighty-eight employees, persons who availed themselves of the program, responded. Of the respondents, 53% indicated being helped by the program. Ninety-three percent indicated they would continue using the program and 96% felt the program would continue. A study of

150 men, averaging 12.7 months in the program showed a 52% attendance improvement, a 74.6% decrease in indemnity costs, and a 55.35% decrease in health, medical and surgical costs (Pontius, p., 17).

McDonnell Douglas Corporation.

Scanlon (1991) reported on a study conducted by Alexander & Alexander Health Strategies Group. The study was done on the EAP of the McDonnell Douglas Corporation (MDC). The study looked at savings to investment ratios. The total cost of the program in 1987 was $2.5 million. The cost in 1988 was $3.9 million. The return on investment in 1987 was 3:1 and rose to 4:1 in 1988. This equates to a $3 dollar return for every dollar invested in 1987 growing to a $4 return for each dollar invested in these programs in 1988. This cost study is of particular importance. Scanlon (1991) states that the study was conducted by an independent third party using accepted scientific methods. At the time of the study, the data base used was the largest to date. The outcomes were studied over a period of time. Alexander and Alexander did not attempt to measure the financial dollars in such a way as it could not be measured objectively and concretely (Scanlon, 1991, pp. 66-67).

Leading the Alexander & Alexander data research team was Dr. Jack Mahoney, Master of Public Health (MPH) and MD. He and his team tried not to have the data contaminated and spent considerable time and effort achieving that end. Regarding the controls employed to protect the integrity of the data:

> Each study subject—both EAP clients and other employees or dependents who were treated for a condition which could have been managed by the EAP- was matched to a cohort control group of 10 other MDC employees on six demographic variables. The variables were age, sex, marital status, geographic location, family size and job code....As we performed the study, we found "contaminated" cases, or those who obtained multiple treatments through both EAP and non-EAP referral channels. These cases were eliminated. We also factored out catastrophic cases, such

as people who received kidney transplants, to keep the cost
data from being skewed (The Almacan, 1989, p. 20).

Further examination of the MDC study brings a clearer
picture in the amount of dollars saved. The results of the 5
year MDC study estimated that in the following 4 years, the
offset value of the program would be $6 million. This includes
a lessening of employee and dependent medical claims by $5.1
million. Absenteeism was predicted to be reduced by 7761 days,
equating to a savings of $900,000.

Because of the size of the MDC, Dr. Mahoney was afforded
the opportunity to match one client to a cohort of 10. This
included dependents as well as employees. The demographic
variables were age, sex, marital status, size of family, geographic
location, and job code.

One of the first things noted was a marked increase in
costs of medical costs for those accessing the program. The
cost more than doubled from $2,000 to over $4,000. The
medical cost for those not accessing the program rose from just
under $2,000 to over $8,000. The cause of the rise is primarily
due to the cost of alcohol treatment. In a three year period
after the inception of the program, the medical expenditures
for the non EAP remained significantly higher that the EAP
group. One explanation for the higher rate is the possibility of
a relapse or other medical complications. Medical expenditures
were slightly higher for EAP clients in the year subsequent to
the program implementation than the year prior to program
implementation. For non EAP clients in the same time period,
the figure was almost double. The study also indicated a greater
medical cost to families of non EAP clients. It appears that
family members of those who do not choose to use the program
are more heavily impacted by the employee's behavior. These
people sought treatment for non mental health conditions.

Despite the apparent increase in medical expenses for the
study period, Dr. Mahoney and his staff show the benefit of the
program. In the area of employee alcoholism, the average per
case medical claim for EAP clients is below that of non EAP

client by $9,898. The average claim for a family of EAP client is lower that the non EAP client by $5,522. Regarding employees with drug problems, the average medical claim was $715 lower than a non EAP client. The family claim for the same category was lower by $7,765. EAP clients with mixed abuse problems average medical claim was $5,779 less than for non EAP clients, with the family claim being lessened by $739. Employees with a psychiatric condition and who are clients of EAP had medical claims of $715 less than the claims of non EAP clients and the family claim was lower by $6,292 (The Almacan, 1989, pp. 18-26).

Department of Health and Human Services.

The private business sector, inclusive of labor unions were not the only people impacted by chemical dependency and mental health issues. The public sector was also suffering from the problems inflicted on business from these problems. The motivation to address these problems came through law, not just knowledge of the cost to industry in production, absenteeism, and treatment. The Comprehensive Alcohol Abuse and Alcoholism Prevention, Treatment, and Rehabilitation act, more commonly known as the Hughes Act, named for its author Senator Harold Hughes, was passed in 1970. The act encouraged assistance programs to deal with the problems of alcohol in the private sector but mandated programs for federal employees. In 1979, the Office of Personnel Management (OPM), the agency charged with overseeing the Hughes Act, issued a letter directing the Federal Civilian Alcohol and Drug Abuse Programs to incorporate personal, emotional, marital, financial and other problems to be part of the program scope. These problems were addressed by the Employee Counseling Services (ECS) of the U.S. Department of Health and Human Services (HHS). To insure an unbiased accounting for the program, HHS contracted with an outside firm, Development Associates, Inc., of Arlington, VA., for evaluation. The evaluation was set up to maximize the assurance of confidentiality and minimize the burden placed on ECS. It required timely feedback and credible results collected on an individual basis. It placed emphasis on both cost and benefits effectiveness. Context, input, process, impact, and outcomes were the five components of the evaluation. The context was the setting within the ECS unit and contained such information like the characteristics of the organization, geographical, physical characteristics and community setting. The input consisted of program resources. It also contained the characteristics of the project and the staff. The process portion included program decision makers having the information related to overcoming procedural problems and the ability to make procedural decisions. It also required interpretation of the program outcomes. Impact required the ability to discover changes on particular, affected employees. These changes were to be in the areas of coping with family issues, work, and health performance. Outcomes were the most important component of the evaluation. In this case the outcomes were measured in the reduction of administrative costs to HHS.

The study included the use of control groups. HHS was divided into 16 units. The units not participating in the study were the control group. Demographics such as sex, age, and salary level were employed. This process allowed for data to be linked to program total costs and costs to each of the individual ECS Units.

The program showed cost effectiveness. Work performance, as gauged by supervisors, rose from -2.5 to +1.3 within six months; the average cost for client served was $951; there was a return of $9 for each $1 spent on the program. Another cost effective outcome was in learning one full time counselor could realize maximum return while dealing with an average of 3500 people per counselor. Cost benefits were also good. Costs per client were $991; for every dollar spent, a return of $1.29 was realized within six months. This analysis showed that for every dollar spent, there would be a return of over $7 (Maiden, 1988, pp., 191-202).

Seagram.

The Seagram Company took a different tack in establishing their employee program. They used professional social workers as a major component of the program. The company contracted with the McGill University School of Social Work to administer the program. Montreal, Quebec Canada was the site of the beginning of the Seagram program. It soon spread to other plants through out Canada, including Amherstburg, Ontario. The company believed that an on-site social work service would deal effectively with employee psychological problems. They also felt the employees would accept the program since it was not run by the company. Soon after expansion there was a disagreement between labor and management over the program. A strike took place at the Amherstburg plant. The program was temporarily suspended. University consultants from the University of Windsor School of Social Workers, responsible for the administration of the Amherstburg program, uncovered a major reason for the labor/management disagreement. The company did not significantly involve the union in the program. The union felt the program was controlled by management and advised the membership not to make themselves available for the program. After visiting and studying many companies with programs, many of which had third party contracts, the program was restarted. This time the company had a five member committee, two from management, two from the union, and the social worker. The formation of the committee helped remove the blocks to service utilization. It gave the employees an opportunity to participate, fully, in the establishment and monitoring of the program.

The newly revised program was expanded to include the broad brush concept of program assistance while keeping the focus on chemical dependency, the main concern of the company. The program also shifted the focus from individual problem identification to one of organizational intervention. The program now includes weekly stress management and weekly relaxation programs. It provides films and speakers for the promotion of good health. Counseling, both on site and referral to outside agencies, was available. All these services were available to family workers as well as employees.

Seagram received an additional benefit in setting up and maintaining the programs by the association with the universities. There was little cost involved. Much of the work was done by students who are required to do research as part of their social work graduate program.

The study took place over an eight year period. This included a four year period before and a four year period subsequent to program implementation. Some demographics employed were employment history, community and family involvement, and help seeking. The social work approach differed in regards to a more traditional program. The demographics of sex, age and salary were not included. The results were favorable. Absentee rates dropped by slightly over 50%. The absentee rate for Seagram was almost 12% annually. Within five years after program implementation, that rate dropped to a low of 5.5%. On-the-job accidents dropped dramatically. In a three year period, they dropped from 562 to 349. Grievances went from 117 to 40 over a four year period, a difference of almost 66%. In the Seagram program satisfaction with the program, as well as success and failure criteria were examined. Ninety four percent of people sampled found the program helpful. Sixty five percent said they would refer others to the program. Seventy eight percent said that if they would use the program if they found the need to do so. 90% said they believed the program could be useful to other companies (Chandler, Kroeker, Flynn, and MacDonald, 1988, pp. 243-253).

Richard L. Peck (1995) reports similar inquires into program satisfaction, similar to the inquiries made in the Seagram program, are recommended. He interviewed Dr. John Bunker, ScD., MHS, a health care consultant for the largest independent human resources consulting firm in the world, The Wyatt Company. Dr. Bunker suggests that questions on the success of a program go beyond utilization data. He feels that satisfaction by a program user is of value. The company providing mental health and substance abuse assistance should know how the recipient of the treatment feels about the program. What was the quality of care? Were you listened to? How long did it take to get an appointment? In general, how do you feel about the program?

<u>General Motors.</u>

Dr. Michael Smith presented testimony to the National Institute of Health (NIH) on May 21, 1993. Along with brief auto-biography and history of the Lincoln Hospital Acupuncture Clinic, he gave testimony on the immense savings realized by General Motors after instituting acupuncture as part of the assistance program. Prior to the implementation of acupuncture as part of substance abuse programs, General Motors was spending more than one billion dollars annually on substance abuse. Most of this money went for inpatient treatment and for relapse related problems. Nicholas Rossano former President of Substance Abuse Recovery of Flint, MI., found that by using acupuncture along with toxicology and psycho-therapy, he could treat people as outpatients for $1170 per patient, per year. General Motors was spending approximately $8000 per patient, per year, for similar outpatient treatment. Rossano showed General Motors how they could save $100 million a year by setting up in-house acupuncture based treatment. The assistance programs would be involved. General Motors tracked the outcomes generated by the Substance Abuse Recovery program. There was an immediate, pronounced improvement. A group of 100 employees was monitored. Eighty-three percent of the group was clean, productive, reliable workers after one year of entering treatment. Of the remaining 17% it was noted that all of them had attended less than 5 visits (Smith, Testimony presented to the NIH Office of Alternative Medicine and the National Wellness Coalition).

<u>University of Michigan.</u>

Another study confirming the value of Employee Assistance Programs was a five year study conducted at the University of Michigan in 1985. The school requested that it's Faculty and Staff Assistance Program conduct a cost benefit study in an effort to justify or vilify the full time EAP staff on the medical campus. The results showed that clients using the Faculty and Staff Assistance Program were absent almost three days less during the time of the study. In an effort to solidify the value of the program operation, a five-year follow up study was recommended in 1992. Thus, this study examined sick leave and retention data on the group studied. The study group was matched against a control group of similar demographics such as education, sex and age, years of service and job categories. The follow up study showed continued cost benefits in the area of absenteeism and in the area of job retention. A comparison of persons leaving the employ of the study group showed that the attrition rate was less than normal rates. Out of the 122 in the original study group, it was expected that 58 or 51% should have remained working. The study showed that 76 or 62% of that group remained employed during the five year study period. The majority of those who left the employ of the medical center during this same five year period appear to have left in favor of career opportunities, school, or family matters. They did not leave for failing to address the issues. The cost saving due to the retention of employees was $35,802. The basis for this figure is the average cost per hire of $1,989 times 18, the number of persons who remained over the average attrition rate. Sick leave for group one, the study group, decreased an average of 5.1 days or 44% from 1989 to 1991. This is in contrast to 9.9 sick days averaged by the entire medical center staff. These figures are based on 57 people in the group of 122. Factored into these figures is a rise in sick leave used by the study group in 1989. The rise in sick time may be due to the fact that in 1988 the institute allowed three additional days for sick care leave for dependent care. There was a parallel increase in sick leave used by all the employees of the medical center subsequent to the implementation of the additional sick time in 1988 (Bruhnsen, 1994, pp. 11 & 27). The study is summarized: Despite some problems in the study design, there is strong evidence that Group 1 employees who used EAP services took less sick leave and were retained in the work force for longer periods of time than the overall medical center staff, all of which resulted in major cost savings to the University of Michigan and continued support for its EAP (Bruhnsen, 1994, p. 27).

Alcohol and Drug Abuse Weekly Report.

Alcoholism and Drug Abuse Weekly (1995), issued a report on a study conducted on 502 adult employees and 508 professionals from the ranks of human resources. This report shows savings in the area of employee replacement. Depending on the employee, from hourly wage earner to senior executives, there is a cost of $7000 to $40,000 for replacement. This report stated that for each dollar spent on programs a loss of $5 to $7 was avoided and absenteeism declined by 66%. A behavioral health program could reduce sick leave by 37%. These figures seem even more important in light of the report showing that of all the companies surveyed only 71% had substance abuse services. The percentage of employees aware of such programs was 42% with just 6% participating in these programs. This report indicates there is an overall benefit to management, labor and, the individual.

UST, Inc.

UST provides a different view in accessing substance abuse and mental health assistance. An employee could access help through the EAP Group or the Medical Plan Group. The significant difference was the support offered to the employee by the two plans. Utilizing the Medical Plan, the employee chose a provider and filed a claim through the company insurance carrier. The employee was on his/her own to find a qualified provider. The system had no control on quality or cost. In essence, the Medical Plan provided financial assistance for the help. The EAP Group made available not only financial assistance but offered a richer benefit design. This included face-to-face assessments and EAP referrals. Also included was a provider network that was carefully chosen. These two methods afforded UST the opportunity to compare costs of a traditional carrier administered benefit and a customized, case driven approach. The study found the EAP Group cost of providing customized care less costly than the Medical Plan. The savings were $1.28 million over the three years in which the study was conducted. The company did not expect to find that providing customized care would be significantly less than care provided by the alternate plan. The results were even more surprising when the study revealed that the number of people in the EAP Group was twice the number of persons in the Medical Plan. The study also noted the increased use of inpatient care for mental health or substance abuse problems by the EAP Group. The focus was on up-front inpatient hospitalization for stabilizing the patient and improving the condition. This was followed by after care that focused on relapse prevention. Despite the increased hospitalization the study found the EAP Group program to be cost effective. Inpatient and outpatient costs for both groups were compared on a per capita basis. The results showed the EAP Group cost to be 80% of the cost of the Medical Plan. Inpatient stays and length of hospital stays dropped steadily over the period of the study for the EAP Group. Meanwhile, there was an overall increase in admission rates for the entire company. A reason for the difference is in noting the EAP Group admission needs were reviewed on a case-by-case basis. This resulted in diverting numerous individuals away from inappropriate medical admissions and toward a more selective mental health and substance abuse treatment, either inpatient or on an outpatient basis. The EAP Group had an inpatient admission rate of less than 50% than that of the Medical Plan. During this same period, the EAP Group had fewer inpatient medical days than its' counterpart. Realizing substance abuse is occasionally treated inadequately, the model used with greater frequency was the one utilizing investing in up-front inpatient care to stabilize and improve the condition. This was followed by after-care focusing on relapse prevention. Because of this approach, the EAP group had higher admission rates for substance abuse, per thousand than the Medical Plan. The cost effectiveness of the EAP Group was indicated when the study disclosed the comparison of inpatient and outpatient claims costs. It was disclosed that the EAP Group inpatient costs were

80% of the costs for the Medical Plan. The outpatient costs were similar. A final indicator of the success and value of the EAP was shown by company action. UST unified the mental health and substance abuse benefits that were provided by the Medical Plan the EAP Group. This was done to strengthen the quality of care for EAP related cases while saving money in both the long and short term.

UST attributes a savings of almost $275,000 in the substance abuse and mental health areas to the customization of the EAP. This took place in the first year, 1994. The increase savings was noted in channeling employees and family members from the Medical Plan Group into the customized EAP (Thormann, 1996, pp. 18 [4]).

Proprietary report study.

I recently was given an unpublished report containing proprietary information. The report was based on results of a recently concluded study by the EAP of a major, international corporation. No financials were issued with the study. It is focused more on the effects the program has in relationship to improved health, both physical and mental. The company is heavily unionized and has a union/management committee. The study was conducted by a group outside the committee but within the company. The union was not involved. There is a possible indicator of employee reluctance to participate in a study without union involvement. The union representing the employees has representation on the assistance program committee and was contacted by the author of this study. The union had no knowledge of the study either being conducted or the results. This study was called an EAP CD Outcome Management System Baseline Report. It was offered to 786 EAP clients. Fifty eight percent refused to participate. Three hundred thirty two people enrolled in the study. The demographics included age, sex, race, marital status, education level, and salary. The client base was not limited to employees but included spouses, children, or other dependents. The ages ranged from 67 to 15 with an average age of 39.3 years. Of the initial 332 clients, 291 or 87.7% were referred to treatment. The treatment modalities included 95 inpatients, 89 intensive outpatients, 40 residential treatments, and 38 outpatients. Partial hospitalization was recommended for 23 clients while 6 were not referred to professional treatment. Alcohol was far and away the most problematic substance as identified by the clients, treatment providers, and case managers. A baseline was created on the health status of the client population, comparing that population to a control group identified as the general population. Concerns with body pain, mental health, general health, social functioning, role limitations due to physical conditions, and vitality were included in the baseline.

A follow up study was done on 74 clients. Role limitations and social functioning were slightly below the average of the general population while body pain, general health, and vitality were even or extremely close to the general population. The mental health aspect increased greatly almost equaling that of the general population. Those not referred to treatment were found to use mental health counseling more than those referred clients. Visits to medical doctors were higher by referred clients. The author of the paper concluded, in conversation with the author of this study, that there is a higher use of medical services due to the awareness of problems that were dismissed by the client through being preoccupied with chemicals. There was a dramatic use of emergency room visits by non-referred, 11% to 89%. Medical-surgical hospital admissions were also dramatically higher for the client who was not referred to treatment, 10% to 90%. During the time of the study, there was no readmission to treatment for 88% of the clients and those that did require readmission reported an 85% reduction in chemical usage. A 15% increase in drug and alcohol use was reported by the 12% who required readmission. The study showed that there was a marked decrease in health expenditures. The majority of the positives were indicated by those clients who used inpatient or residential treatment programs as compared to the results shown by those clients who used outpatient treatment.

The Proprietary Study was conducted to determine the future of the assistance programs in the company. The company looked at results such as hospital emergency room usage and medical-surgical hospital admissions. Referred program participants use of these services was much less than non-referred participants. It also looked at the small percentage of readmissions to treatment for referred participants compared to the non-referred participants. Upon reviewing these results the company decided to retain the program.

Chamberlain Contractors results.

Chamberlain Contractors is a small, Laurel, Maryland based asphalt paving company with a payroll of approximately 70 employees. Despite having a payroll less than the average of a rural community company (80), Chamberlain does not fit into the category of a rural company. It is in close proximity to Washington, DC., and the city of Baltimore, MD. The workers' compensation cost to the company was nearly $100,000 a year. On-the-job injuries and vehicular accidents were extremely high. Two years after setting up their assistance program the costs dropped to $22,000. There was not one on-the-job injury or vehicular accident (Drugs in the Workplace, 1997, p. 6). Another report shows the same positive effect with different figures. The cost of the EAP was $7,000 a year. They provided alcohol and drug safety awareness programs. Chamberlain supplements its EAP with drug testing. The testing is done before employment, randomly and after accidents. Workers' Comp and liability costs were reduced by $50,000. The cost of health insurance premiums leveled off as did accidents where substance abuse was involved (Gemignani, 1997).

Other results.

As a result of assistance programs, studies conducted by the New York Transit Authority claim a saving of $1 million in paid sick leave benefits, for one year. AT&T claimed actual and anticipated savings of $448,000 while the then New York Telephone Company claimed $1.5 million in savings. General

Motors stated it realized savings as shown by a 72% reduction in the dollars paid out for accident and sickness disabilities (Scanlon, 1991, p., 72).

In an effort to gather more hard data on absenteeism, reduction of on-the-job accidents, and improved overall attendance, I sought the advice and direction of several experts in the EAP/MAP field. Calls were placed to the research departments of the AFL/CIO, both nationally and on a state level. Another call was placed to the research department of Employees Assistance Professional Association. All three offices responded by saying the data sought is very rare. Each organization suggested seeking this information from the other. Ted Mapes, C.A.C., LAP-C, Past President of the New York City Chapter of LAP, Former National President and founder of Labor Assistance Professionals, Former Director of MAP services for local 100 of the Transportation Workers Union, and Labor Chair for EAPA states that his local does not keep records regarding that type of data. He checked with other LAP members and found they also do not retain this type of data. Mr. Mapes said he requested this data from the New York City Transit Authority, the employer. Each request was denied (Ted Mapes, personal communication, Jan. 1998). Ben LoCasto, CSW, CEAP, previously a manager for Employee Advisory Services at Metropolitan Life. Previously, Mr. LoCasto was the Director of EAP Services for the Long Island Railroad. Mr. LoCasto stated he was approached by the upper level management of the railroad about having a study that would indicate how much money was saved in areas such as accident and disability reduction, improved work production and reduction in over all absenteeism. They suggested a study similar to the MDC. When Mr. LoCasto told his superiors the cost of such a study, in excess of $2 million, they scrubbed the idea. Mr. LoCasto maintains the cost of such a study is the primary reason studies of this nature are not being conducted (Ben LoCasto, personal communication, Jan. 1998). I looked for other sources. I turned to academics for possible leads toward uncovering this sought information. I spoke with William Sonnenstuhl and Peter Bamberger. These gentlemen teach Labor Courses at Cornell University, co-author books on MAPs, and are affiliated with the Smithers Institute. Both these gentlemen stated that the hard data being sought was almost non-existent. Mr. Sonnenstuhl states that he is currently awaiting a grant for the purpose of conducting the research that may uncover what is currently being searched (Sonnenstuhl and Bamberger, personal communication, Jan. 1998). Walter Scanlon, C.A.C., CEAP, M.B.A., is the author of a prime source of research in this study. He is also self-employed as an EAP consultant, and a teacher. Scanlon agrees with the others, including Walter Reichman, Ph. D., the head of the Psychology Department, Baruch School, City College of New York. There is a great lack of hard data (Scanlon and Reichman, personal communication, Jan. 1998). They all agree that a possible deterrent to finding all encompassing data is the very high cost of such studies. All the above mentioned individuals and organizations recommend the study of MDC as the premier example of hard data. Only Dr. Reichman, William Sonnenstuhl, and Peter Bamberger seemed to be aware of the University of Michigan study and the study of Seagram. What these gentlemen all have in common is they believe management is no longer looking for hard data. Peck, (1995) reports through his interview with Dr. Bunker that people paying for treatment want results at a reasonable rate. They want to know if behavioral care is offsetting the cost of medical care. They want to know how productive an employee is after treatment. Bunker goes on to relate that most employers are not developing this data as of yet but it is of interest to them. This coincides with my conversation with Sonnenstuhl and his seeking a grant to research this data.

All programs do not work.

Since programs are created for and by humans and taking into consideration humans are fallible, all programs do not work. There are also those who do not wish to have EAPs as part of their everyday workplace

General Motors Corporation Oldsmobile Division.

Comparing the in depth study of GM Canada against the Oldsmobile Division, one can find a glaring disparity. The Oldsmobile Division used 13 more employees and provided less information. The study claimed to be successful in reporting reductions in absences, accidents, grievances, and in the payment of sickness and accident benefits. The study, however, admitted to failing in following up on all participants (Pontius, p. 18). Despite being an early program, preceding the Oldsmobile study, and the fact there was little hard core data, the Baltimore Union/Management study, in 1972, provided more pertinent information. The Oldsmobile report covered one year while the Baltimore study covered a two year period. Baltimore reported savings in dollars for the two years of the study along with a geometric projection for further savings. It also included a savings due to increased morale and less equipment damage. In comparing the Oldsmobile study against the Baltimore study there appears to be a difference in depth and focus. This paper also notes the GM Canada study was much more inclusive.

Rural programs.

Most of the studies cited in the report were from large organizations that were primarily located in or close to large metropolitan areas. What they had in common was they showed a positive effect on the company bottom line. The company saved money as a result of programs. Programs seem to be advantageous but there are times when they do not serve the needs of the business, especially businesses located in rural communities.

The figure for a population defining a rural community is broad. The U.S. Census Bureau defines a rural community as one with a population of 2500. The bureau defines a metropolitan area as one with a population of 50,000. A rural community has been perceived as one with traditional lifestyles, strong family orientation, fundamentally religious, and resistant to outside influences. They usually have limited mental, medical, and social services. Over the past 20 years there has been a migration of people and business, southward. Despite this migration, there is little data on EAPs in rural communities. A study regarding the movement of business to a rural area of central Louisiana and the use of EAPs was conducted.

Fifteen companies were sampled. Among the samples were automobile manufacturers, a public utility, a retail discount store and locally owned businesses. Consultation was sought from professionals in that area who had knowledge of programs. Of the 15 businesses only 40% (6) had an EAP. Five were in the process of developing a program while the remaining 7 did not have a program. Of the 6 with programs, 5 were unionized employers. One was totally non-union. Each of the 6 companies employed between 300 and 3,000 people, averaging 1500 employees. Four of the 6 programs stated that there was no need for improvement in their program. The remaining 2 programs saw removing confidentiality and lowering program cost as necessary as well as desired improvements. The employer with no program had an average of 80 employees. These companies said if an employee presented a problem it would represent grounds for dismissal. At best the employee would be asked to sign a last chance letter. All the programs provided services other than drug and alcohol assistance. Some included service in marital, emotional, and financial matters. The internal services were usually provided by a staff doctor or nurse. Mental health and social work issues were handled externally.

The major reason attributed to not having programs available to most, if not all employees in the area, is the large available worker pool. The particular area studied in the report had 5 major state universities and one private university in relatively close proximity. The students along with local housewives provided an abundant labor supply that lent itself to the part time needs of many of the businesses. There was also the turnover-in-employment rate to be considered before implementing an assistance program. Sometimes it is just not worth the cost to implement, staff, or pay for such benefits (Dicks, 1988, pp. 255-264).

Undisclosed Firm.

A firm in Canada having 9,000 employees began an assistance program in 1976. A committee was formed with the responsibility of creating and monitoring the program. The committee was comprised of two union and two management officials. They could not agree on an addictions counselor and went to an out side agency for the counselor. Participation in the program was mandatory. The study from between June, 1976 through December, 1983. By the end of the study, 19 of the 61 participants still had their cases open. Of the 42 that were closed, 38% or 23 were reopened during the study. The 38% reopening rate was significantly higher than the reopen rate of the outside firm conducting the study. This suggested that many of the closed cases may still be reopened. Despite these findings the company felt the program to be successful and continued to adhere to its' mandatory referral policy (Wright, 1988, pp. 206 – 210).

Summary

When I decided to attempt writing on this subject, I found the information to make or break my views on the success of assistance programs was scattered. This was discussed earlier. I hope the information contained in this chapter serves the needs and curiosity of many. There are other studies available if someone wants to dig them up. There should be enough here to satisfy the curious and those in need of data for the purpose of research.

Assistance programs work. If they did not, they would not be in existence in the workplace. They would probably still be a part of labor unions but the professionalism of the union personnel would not be pushed to the level of experience and education that they enjoy today. In all fairness, there was a need to look at programs that were less than successful. If they were not successful, it could be important to find out why. In discussing the lack of success in rural areas and small companies

I do not want to give the impression that all small companies do not embrace EAPs or MAPs. This will be visited later. It is sufficient to say that programs work.

What some may find interesting is the different approach and outcomes uncovered in the various studies. The Navy study found the rate of success in their program to be more successful with the older, more career oriented serviceman. MDC showed several different results. This is because the company spent millions on the study. They had plenty of human subject material as witnessed by their wide use of employee demographics. One interesting fact uncovered was the doubling of medical costs for those who successfully used the assistance program while those who did not avail themselves of the program had their medical costs quadruple. The HHS showed that EAPs and MAPs are not limited to the private sector. Seagram showed innovative talent in their hiring of Social Workers and Social Work Graduate Students. It was cheaper and gave a different view of the workplace. They used different demographics. General Motors employed acupuncture as part of their program. The University of Michigan Study focused on job retention. UST rolled both their programs into the more successful EAP while the Undisclosed Firm focused their EAP study on the improved mental and physical health of the employee.

Throughout all the studies examined, successful and less than successful, the one constant is still evident. People and the bottom line.

CHAPTER 6

Before we can look at the importance of unions taking care of their own through MAPs or UAPs it might be helpful to take a look at the past and the efforts of many to stop people from drinking or at least curb their excessive drinking. We will see that despite the many attempts, nothing has worked. The alternative is to help. We aren't going to stop cultural or religious pasts where alcohol was and is a part of society and we are certainly not going to stop addiction but we can help.

Past Attempts At Assistance

Throughout history we have seen notice being given concerning the excesses of alcohol. Biblical Scholars can point pout many passages in both the Old and New Testaments of warnings about alcohol. We've seen some of the previous subtle warnings but really strong movements against alcohol didn't take place until the late 18th and early 19th centuries. We saw Neoloin and Handsome Lake begin movements using some of the principles in use today.

Previously mentioned were Benjamin Rush and Anthony Benezet. We know that drinking was viewed as an acceptable method of communal bonding and we have previously seen that it came under attack in the latter part of the 18th century. The abstinence movement took on a religious fervor by 1811 and workplace drinking began to come under attack from the religious community. The attack was spearheaded by two important figures of that time, Dr. Benjamin Rush, referred to as the father of American Psychiatry and a signer of the

Declaration of Independence, and Anthony Benezet, a wealthy Philadelphia Quaker. In addressing the annual general assembly of the Presbyterian Church in Philadelphia, PA., Rush, asked the clergy to take the position of favoring temperance based on theological reasoning (Lender & Martin, p. 66). Their reasoning for the attack was also a moral issue, not one that was business orientated. They argued that the consumption of distilled spirits was destroying the moral order. They advocated temperance, not abstinence. The true meaning of abstinence, in this example, is the non-consumption of any alcoholic beverage. Temperance is allowing the consumption of certain alcoholic beverages which are classified as non-distilled beverages. Beverages such as beer and wine fall into the non-distilled beverage category (Bacharach, et al, p. 8). The approach to alcohol consumption served the purpose of Rush and Benezet. Their primary concern was alcohol use as an issue of morality not solely a workplace issue. They were interested in reshaping the morality of the nation by banning ardent spirits. Their railing against the use of alcohol by workers helped foster their mission. There were, however, those who, at that time, advocated for total abstinence. Again, the reasoning was not moral or socially based. Lender & Martin (1987) tell us these reformers were interested in saving individuals from the fate of an alcoholic life style. The alcoholic life style also was often one of losing a job or income due to drinking. This shift broadened the ever widening gap between the employer and the worker. This spawned the need for workers to protect themselves. Prior to the Industrial Revolution, the craftsman and apprentice worker worked closely. The Industrial Revolution often saw the master craftsman becoming the employer and the apprentice as an employee. A successful master craftsman would turn his workshop into a factory, forever altering the relationship of craftsman and apprentice or journeyman. This new alignment caused tensions which remain to the present day. This combined with the appearance of temperance and abstinence movements helped mark the beginning of the first self-help groups, job based groups that later evolved into employer and union based assistance programs (Bacharach, et al, p. 7; Lender & Martin, pp. 69 & 74).

In 1840, the previously mentioned A/A prototype group known as the Washingtonians was formed by 6 men from Baltimore. The carried out public meetings but the public grew tired of their agitation suggesting that they, too, were advocating for total abstinence. Before that, in 1826, The American Society for the Promotion of Temperance was founded. By 1833 there were over 1000 chapters with more than one million members. Their campaign was directed against using spirits. Their proposal to include all alcoholic drinks was rejected by most in 1833 but somehow was accepted in 1836 and remains to date. By the mid 1830s the American Temperance Society had over 200,000 members.

Probably the most famous temperance movement leader in the US was Susan B. Anthony. Not only was she heavily involved in temperance movements she was involved in the women's rights movement headed by Elizabeth Cady Stanton and Amelia Bloom in the mid 19th century. Despite being elected President of Rochester, NY branch of the Daughters of Temperance, she was denied the right to speak at the convention of the Sons of Temperance and in 1853 formed, along with Stanton, the Women's State Temperance Society. They advocated for legislation limiting the sale of alcohol (Susan B. Anthony House, 2006). One might conclude that these two avid proponents of temperance, by virtue of seeking limitations on the sale of alcohol, realized that total temperance was not to be achieved.

Temperance movements did not just focus on the drinkers of the day they actively sought to stop the production and sale of spirits. By 1873 Dr. Diocletian Lewis a professional lecturer was advising women, through his lectures, to strive toward getting local community dispensers of alcohol to stop the sale of alcoholic beverages. Through the winter of 1874, the parades of women protesting the making and distribution of alcoholic beverages drove the liquor business out of 250 towns. Over 900 marches took place in 31 states. In some instances the saloon keepers loosed dogs on the marchers while at other locations they were attacked by brewers. Temperance wasn't going to solve the problems caused by, at that time, the unknown disease of alcoholism. By the end of the 19th century, Chicago, IL, had as many saloons as the number of grocery, meat, and dry goods stores, combined.

I will not bore you with probably the biggest failure in legislating or religiously dictated temperance, the National Prohibition Act, or Volstead Act of 1919. Movies and television shows about Prohibition, Scarface Al Capone, and Eliot Ness are available. What these forms of entertainment do not show is what they have in common with all the other Temperance Movements; none of the probably well intended movements would or could not stop people from drinking and certainly did nothing to stem the tide of alcohol addiction.

Unions: Why they help?

Earlier, Leo Perlis was mentioned along with his belief in the broad brush approach to assistance. Leo was the social conscience of Organized Labor. It was his dream that Organized Labor champion the causes of society. Responsible for the founding of the Community Services Arm of the AFL-CIO, Leo had the ear and support of one of the greatest cross sections of Americana, from people in the political arena like Eleanor Roosevelt, Harry Truman, Lyndon Johnson, Eunice Shriver, Ted and Bobby Kennedy, Hubert Humphrey, to people like Jonas Salk, Danny Kaye, Jerry Lewis and union leaders like Phil Murray, Joe Beirne, Walter Reuther, George Meany, right down to the union workers who fulfilled his dream He is also noted for his concept of the 'Human Contract'. The Human Contract, in a nutshell, was that unions were responsible for taking care of problem of the membership that weren't covered by a collective bargaining agreement. This is a continuation of the Cordwainers assisting their members and families almost two hundred years in the past. Almost every Union Assistance Program I ever come across was started, built, maintained, and continues to operated by and through Union Brothers and Sisters in recovery from addictions, part of the Human

Contract.. But is it addictions that drive us toward helping our less fortunate brothers and sisters and their families? Is it our duty to help those who need us? Is it our heritage, our traditions that leads us toward helping? It certainly isn't the salaries and most definitely not the hours dedicated to operating and maintaining a successful program, providing services 24/7, 365. The answer to the questions is all.

There are other compelling reasons why unions help. Other people that we have come to believe have the skills and knowledge to provide assistance in this area, have a record that tells us they don't often help. Most doctors, 82%, avoid addressing alcoholism in their patients. The families of the alcoholic want their doctors to intervene in some way. Seventy-two percent of all families where the doctor has not intervened say they wanted their doctor to intervene. Management does not, necessarily, get involved with identifying an alcoholic worker on their initiative. We know they will work with a union counterpart and maybe with a peer in a non union environment but 58% are reluctant to act solo. Oddly enough, that percentage carries over to the clergy. Fifty-eight percent of clergy admit that they do not offer assistance in addressing alcohol as a problem, even when counseling families (Hart, 1998). In my mind these latest figures fosters an even greater need for unions to continue to provide assistance for members and their families.

By 2001 there was an increase of over 5000 new Union Assistance Programs, much of it brought on by the introduction of Managed Care and Drug Testing. A result of the introduction of Managed Care and Drug Testing lead to management looking to take shortcuts which included firing rather than rehabilitation. Fact-to-Face evaluations were being replaced with 800 numbers where the diagnosis and recommendation for treatment were made by people on the other end of an 800 telephone number, miles if not on the other side of the nation. Of course, out patient treatment was usually recommended. Unions recommended in-patient treatment, a course of treatment that has been shown to be more effective. Managed Care often state that their people were professionals with varying degrees, therefore better qualified to made treatment recommendations. This leads to the Labor attempt to better educate its Member Assistance People. This will be discussed later. For now I'll just refer to some of the union people I mentioned earlier, Ted Mapes, Mickey Diamond and Jack Hennessy, who were joined by other union MAPs, Tom Burns, and Don Perks attended a meeting at the Cornell Club in May 2001. Others in attendance were academics William Sonnenstuhl, Samuel Bacharach, and Peter Bamberger. Helping members was the primary focus of the meeting with an emphasis on the issues with Managed Care (Robbins, 2001). It is no coincidence that most of the union program people in attendance are responsible for the founding of LAP and for initiating the LAP-C credentialing educational program.

Summary

We have seen how people and organizations attempted to stem the tide of excessive drinking. We have looked at a myriad of motivational reasons for getting people to stop. We've tried religion, the banning of alcohol, attempts to stop or at least lessen consumption on the job. We know that firing an alcoholic is not the answer, since we know that well over 90% of alcoholics and approximately 75% of all drug abusers are employed. They may get fired but most will eventually find other employment, bringing an often temporarily camouflaged problem to their new employer. We, hopefully, have seen that either a peer or combined effort of assistance offering is often the answer to the problem. Keep in mind that the job is usually the last bastion of the alcoholic or drug addict. They will lose their car, home, family, but the job is usually the last straw and that is where assistance not just total discipline comes into play.

CHAPTER 7

Many people, when they hear of rehabilitation facilities or hospitals, they think of the Betty Ford Clinic or Day Top. These two institutions have certainly received a lot of publicity over the past decades. The Betty Ford Clinic could be described as a Treatment Center while Day Top is a Therapeutic Community. Both provide residential treatment. Day Top is usually much longer, often taking 6 months to 2 years. Betty Ford provides more traditional treatment lasting several weeks, not much longer than 30 days. Of course, these numbers do not hold true across the board. The stay can be longer or shorter. We will take a look at the types of treatment available. Day Top and Betty Ford are far from being the only providers of their respective treatments. Treatment provision is a growing industry commanding a lot of money. Everyone does not go into a residential facility. For the greater majority of employees who are serviced by an EAP or an MAP, treatment in a Therapeutic Community is rare. If there is insurance paying for treatment, the employee is likely to receive treatment in surroundings discussed in this chapter. This chapter also looks at the history of substance abuse benefits, and the cost of providing these benefits. It also addresses some measures that are being taken in an effort to reduce the cost of providing treatment while still maintain quality treatment.

Health Care Benefits and Treatment

History of Substance Abuse Benefits.

It has been previously noted that AA is slightly over 60 years of age. Health care benefits are over 50 years of age. According to Michael McDonald, Master of Vocational Counseling, Certified Alcohol Counselor, past president of the New York Federation Alcohol Counselors, and teacher of counseling techniques at Hofstra University in New York, health benefits, as we know them today, began to appear during World War Two. Mr. McDonald states that in an interview he had with Brinkley Smithers, founder of the Smithers Institute, a chemical dependency facility in New York City, health care benefits began with DuPont & Co. Mr. Smithers maintained that some kind of health benefit was needed to keep employees in the workplace. Jobs were plentiful. A person could find a well paying job at almost any location. Health care benefits were looked at as an attractive addition to a decent salary. As an adjunct to health care, DuPont established the first known multi-plant alcoholism program (Michael McDonald, personal communication, May, 1997).

There is another thought on the emergence of programs to assist workers who have an alcohol problem.

> Controversy lingers over which companies first did what within the conceptual framework of occupational alcoholism. However, most people in the field agree that 1942 through 1944 were benchmark years in which *formal* employee alcoholism programs began in a dozen major manufacturing organizations (Bickerton, 1988, p. 316).

While DuPont is recognized as an early leader in treating alcoholics, they are far from the first. Industrial employers like the Armour Meatpacking Company, McCormick Harvester, and the Chicago Tribune responded to problems related to on-the-job drinking by sending their employees to treatment centers like the Keeley Center for treating alcohol problems, established in 1879 (Lender & Martin, p. 108; Steele, p. 430).

World War Two provided an oxymoron concerning hiring. The war took millions of men and women from the work place. The armed services were depleting the work force of qualified, experienced workers. To foster the needs of the war effort in relationship to mass production, workers who would never have been considered employable were hired. There was a need for alcohol programs in the work place. Since it would be ten more years before alcoholism was declared a disease, the programs tended to be quite informal with the topic of alcoholism being tactfully avoided (Bickerton, 1990, p. 36). Scanlon (1991) said that during that time period, there was a great need of manpower. He also attributes the inception and growth of alcohol programs to the support of medical directors who actively initiated alcohol programs.. Bickerton (1990) tells us that from these early beginnings of occupational programs, it would take another 10 years before alcoholism would be recognized as a disease. In 1956 the American Medical Association said that alcoholism is a disease. This gave alcohol programs a recognized status. Oddly enough, it took the American Medical Association 152 years longer than Dr. Thomas Trotter to conclude that alcoholism is a disease. Trotter, a physician in Edinburgh, Scotland, also concluded that alcohol abuse was detrimental to health in 1804. He maintained that drunkenness was a disease that caused actions and movements within the body resulting in the disorder of health functions. By the 1830s there were movements in New York, Massachusetts, and Connecticut for the hospitalization of drunks in lieu of placing them in jails or workhouses. At approximately the same time Benjamin Rush also wrote about the negative effects on health due to alcohol abuse. Rush was not just known as the father of American psychiatry, he was a signer of the Declaration of Independence and a former Surgeon General of the Army. Even before Trotter and Rush, there is mention of alcoholism as an illness. Drinking problems were not referred to as alcoholism. That is a relatively new word and term. In the 1930s, Richard Peabody began applying psychological methods in treating alcoholics. He also replaced the words drunk and drunkenness with the words alcoholic and alcoholism. He felt these new terms were less judgmental. However, a difference between a person who is intoxicated and a habitual drunkard was noted as far back as the third century BCE. A Roman jurist, in a commentary on imperial law, suggested that an inveterate drunkard be considered as a medical problem and not a legal one. Hospitalization for habitual drunks was recommended by James I of Aragon (Kinney & Leaton, 1978, pp. 17-20). In 1990 the American Society of Addiction Medicine (ASAM) and the National Council on Alcoholism and Drug Dependence (NCADD) revised the definition of "alcoholism" calling it a primary chronic disease with psychological and environmental factors influencing its development (Scanlon, 1991, p. 8). As important as the need for man power and the increased support of programs by medical directors was the rapid growth of Alcoholics Anonymous.

Within a period of approximately 30 years, 75% of Blue Cross Blue Shield policies had some type of alcoholism coverage. Insurance coverage for alcohol treatment did not come easy. Someone had to pay increased premiums. Unions would have to bargain for this extra benefit. Those not represented had to count on the EAPs within their organizations to find a way to get this benefit. One unique twist in the search for paid insurance benefits for alcohol treatment came in the state of Illinois. Kemper Insurance had its' people lobby the government of their state in an effort to have this benefit paid for. Illinois became the first state to mandate coverage for alcoholism in group health insurance policies (Bickerton, 1990).

Not long after the first formal EAPs had been developed in1942 and 43 at DuPont and Eastman Kodak, assistance programs began to grow. In 1945 the Medical College of Cornell University teamed up with Caterpillar Tractor to develop a company-wide mental health program that included dealing with alcoholism (Bickerton, 1990, p. 36). By 1959 there were 50 major companies with programs in place. By 1973 there were 500 programs. By 1984 there were 8000 employee assistance programs in existence. Professional Base Ball, Foot Ball and

Basket Ball teams had some kind of EAP available. By 1991 there were more than 20,000 Employee Assistance Programs in operation. These programs did not only address chemical dependency problems, they addressed other problems troubling the employee.

Treatment alternatives

Another part of the overall question is in finding the proper treatment for the employee or member. What types of treatment are available? Do they work?

As with most things in life, there are choices. A company or union can opt not to implement any type of employee or member assistance program. That particular choice does not seem to fit the needs of a business or the profile of the unions. There are alternatives.

Alcoholics Anonymous.

Success can be measured from an old-stand-by of both member and employee assistance programs, Alcoholics Anonymous (AA). Alcoholics Anonymous is an organization that has been in existence for over 60 years. The birthday of AA is June 10, 1935, reportedly the first day of Bob Smith's permanent sobriety. Bob Smith, otherwise known as Dr. Bob, was one of the co-founders of Alcoholics Anonymous. Its purpose is to help those who want to be sober, stay sober. The AA program espouses abstinence and a type of spirituality among its many tenets. It is not a medical or religious organization but does cooperate with people in the religious and medical communities. AA is quite often recommended by both EAPs and MAPs. It is free and has a successful track record in the treatment of alcoholism. Today's view of treatment may be one of hospitalization or outpatient therapy. AA treats its members differently, by supporting the individual. Several assistance programs have their roots in AA. They will be discussed later.

AA is not 100% successful but does say it has a fine record. Given the fact that the key word in this program or fellowship as AA is referred to, is 'anonymous', it is impossible to amass completely accurate data. AA claims that 50% of those who really wanted to get sober, tried and stuck with the program, remained that way. AA claims that another 25% remained sober after relapsing. A relapse in is when a person resumes drinking after a period of abstinence. Alcoholics Anonymous also claims that those people who tried a few meetings and left, eventually returned at the rate of two out of three (Alcoholics Anonymous, 1976, p. XX).

This option is still recommended by EAPs and MAPs as a source of help for alcoholics. The process begun by the founders Bill Wilson and Dr. Bob, has been adopted by other self help groups The process known as self-help has broadened its scope to include such groups as Overeaters Anonymous, Narcotics Anonymous, Cocaine Anonymous and Gamblers Anonymous, to name some. The idea is the same. Persons suffering from these or other afflictions can get help to remain abstinent from such behavior by getting support from people with the same addiction. Many believe that in unity there is a certain strength. AA and these other anonymous groups provide that unity. They lend their strengths to one another's assistance. The anonymous programs believe in the power of example. These programs have one component that is extremely important to unions and management in the area of cost benefits. They are free.

Outpatient treatment.

When an individual enters the treatment system, several avenues of treatment opportunities are available. There is out-patient treatment where the person attends counseling sessions in a non confined atmosphere. These sessions are usually held in a counselor's or therapist's office. They can also be held on the worksite. The number of sessions per week or month is determined by the counselor. This is usually the most cost efficient option.

Day hospitalization treatment.

There is a day hospitalization treatment wherein the patient spends most of the day in a hospital setting, only to be released in the evening. As with outpatient treatment the length of treatment is determined by the counseling personnel. This option is less costly than inpatient treatment.

Intensive outpatient treatment.

In between these two options is intensive out-patient care. It is not a stringent as day hospital treatment but is more intensive than out-patient treatment. Intensive out-patient treatment could be two or more sessions in one day. There could be anywhere from two to five days in one week for intensive outpatient treatment.

Inpatient treatment.

Inpatient treatment is the most intensive of all the treatment modalities. It is held in a hospital type surrounding. Prior to being admitted to an in-patient facility, the patient is usually confined to a hospital for detoxification. An in-patient rehabilitation facility can have a fully accredited detoxification unit within the facility. The detoxification period can last from one to seven days. Here the patient receives a medical examination conducted by a physician. The duration of time spent in detoxification is often at the discretion of the physician and is motivated by the health of the patient. Another determinant to the length of stay is the effects of withdrawing for the substance or substances at issue. Psychiatric or psychological evaluation is usually conducted. The patient is under the care of nurses. This time does not count toward time in rehabilitation. The cost of detoxification comes through the hospitalization benefit, not the mental health benefit. After detoxification the patient may spend up to 28 days going through the rehabilitation process. Upon discharge, aftercare treatment is strongly recommended. Aftercare is usually counseling sessions, either group, one on one, or both. It is a follow up or continuation of the in-patient treatment. Aftercare should not be confused with out-patient treatment.

All three treatment modalities place great emphasis on attending the self-help group meeting such as AA in addition to whatever treatment method they have been exposed to.

Benefit of inpatient over other treatment.

A study conducted by Medstat Sys. Inc. reported that those who received treatment for 15 to 24 days were readmitted to treatment at the rate of 15.5%, within six months of initial treatment. This was almost twice the readmission rate of those who were treated for longer periods of time (Scanlon, 1991, p. 65).

Treatment of chemical dependence is often quite complex. Many believe the chemically dependent individual needs to know about the disease concept and the issues surrounding relapsing. The individual needs to learn how to self-monitor and to be aware. As with many other things in chemical dependency treatment, this takes time. It is an educational process.

There are physical dysfunctions that accompany chemical dependency. The physical illnesses displayed do not have to be the obvious type of illness. It can be manifested in areas of lack of sleep or maintaining attention. The sleep problems can last up to two years. There can be problems with the thought processes. All these problems take time to address.

Treatment is often referred to as a "program". Recovery is not a program but a process, and process is on going. Programs have a beginning and an end. Like the "journey of a thousand miles", recovery usually has a beginning and that beginning is prior to inpatient or some type of intensive outpatient treatment surrounding. It usually begins with doubts or questions about drinking or drug abuse. The addict may ask himself or herself questions or may become concerned with their problem. The initial questions or concerns can be generated form other sources like family, friends, or the work place. The process has begun. The addict or alcoholic realizes that there may be a problem but what they really want to accomplish is to learn how to control their drinking or drugging. The addicted person will hopefully seek the advice or assistance of a counselor or therapist. These professionals can help the addicted person identify the problem, to assist the person in self-diagnosis. Before the active treatment phase can occur, this must be achieved.

In treatment the patient allows the counselor to steer life in a different direction. The counselor needs to provide clear, solid, and simple directions. The addict needs to have a regimen created. The patient has to learn to make decisions without the pall of dependency hanging in the background. It is difficult at best. For many, the decision making process has been subdued by chemicals for years. The counselor has to make sure that things are clear and unfettered. All this takes a great deal of time. When the patient is released from a facility or from participating in intense outpatient therapy, the process continues with continuing care. This care can be administered by attending therapy on a less stringent level, utilize self help groups like AA or a combination of both. The point being is that the process never stops (Kinney & Leaton, 1978, pp. 134-137).

Paying for and accessing treatment

The MDC program showed there was a benefit to the employer in providing assistance programs. The savings went from $ 3 return on each dollar spend on assistance programs to $4 to $1 in one year. HHS showed a gain of $1.29 to 1$ to as high as gaining $9 for every dollar spent on assistance programs.

Even though they achieved a positive, we should look at the cost of providing the treatment.

Accessing assistance through the use of health care benefits.

AA and its related groups are not the only way management and unions get help for troubled employees or members. Today, many use the benefits provided by health care insurance package. Benefits for substance abuse and mental health issues were not always available. This benefit had to go through a growth period.

The cost of Assistance programs

It may appear that the true beneficiaries of assistance programs are the employees. That is not completely true. Companies also reap benefits. Scanlon (1991) writes that organizations that have invested in assistance programs know that the programs will continue receiving some type of return.

> When one considers the successful alcoholism recovery rate of employees referred to EAPs-some organizations claim as high as 75%-the value of the EAP is evident. Many employees who probably would have eventually lost their jobs, their families, and perhaps their lives have been provided an opportunity to seek treatment and become productive employees once again. Since the population the EAP benefits is within the organization, it follows that the organization ultimately benefits (Scanlon, 1991, p. 24).

Here the social value of assistance programs is brought into light. Assistance programs do help in the social vein while providing a benefit for the employer. Managers as well as unions are aware that there is a return of investment as well as a return of an employee. What they want to know is what is the investment costing.

Foster Higgins conducted a survey of companies with over 5,000 employees and found that psychiatric and substance abuse benefit costs were escalating at an alarming rate. In

1988 the cost increase was 27% and rose to 47% in 1989 with calculated estimated cost of $1.75 million for substance abuse and psychiatric benefits alone by 1992 (Scanlon, 1991, p. 54). The cost for a typical 28 day stay in a rehabilitation center for chemical dependency varied. The cost can waver between $5,000 and $30,000 for the stay. This does not include a detoxification period (Scanlon, 1991, p. 87). There is a high success rate of those who sought help through their EAP rather than face disciplinary action for poor or deteriorating job performance. The estimated rate is 50%. This translates into half of all recipients of EAP services are returned to full production capabilities within one year (Scanlon, 1991, p. 69). Steelcase Inc. located in Grand Rapids, Michigan report that their employees are entering drug treatment programs at the rate of one for each two and one half days at a cost of between $9,000 and $12,000 per person (Bahls, 1998, p., 81). The cost can be figured on the rate of 146 persons getting treatment costing between $1,314,000 to $1,752,000, annually.

Treatment for mental health problems and substance abuse is expensive. In light of the available data it appears that it is worth it. Keeping in mind that programs work, we must not lose focus on the cost. Something needs to be done to reduce the cost of providing treatment. Lower costs help both management and the unions. In bargaining a contract, the union would like to put more money it the pocket of the dues paying members. Reducing medical costs could help in that area. considering the costs are rising more rapidly in the mental health area, it would behoove both union and management to investigate methods of reducing the costs while still maintaining good treatment.

Saving money by changing traditional program methods

Most parties have seen the data, much of which has been gathered in the 1970s and 1980s. This is not meant to indicate data has not been updated, as evidenced in the data recorded in this study, data compiled after 1990. What companies want to know today is if they are saving money through the use of programs and how can they retain successful programs while reducing the cost of those programs?

Company A and Case Management

Employers are looking at how programs affect their bottom line. If they can find ways of increasing or keeping the line from eroding further, they will pursue that end. To assist in helping their bottom line, many employers have turned to Utilization Review Programs (URPs). URPs work separately from EAPs. They are characterized by their use of the telephone consultations and second opinions as the primary method of generating savings. The people and organizations providing medical services offer discounts if employers or carriers use their facilities or networks, exclusively. In the area of mental health and chemical dependency, major EAP issues such as, appropriate treatment, quality care, and the effectiveness of treatment ore often ignored. URPs provide little or no commitment toward the needs of the organization contracting their services. Often there is no opportunity for preventive services that can be based on the data accumulated by the URPs. Diagnostic Related Groups (DRGs), are similar to URPs. They provide

An alternative to these models has been developed by the Professional Employee Advisement Program. It combines EAP with Case Management (EAP/CM). In order for this combination to be effective, several things must happen. 1. The EAP must be separate from preferred provider networks, health care companies, and the contracting organization. It should be autonomous. On the other hand, an EAP cannot be a resource for a treatment provider. A resource provider relationship between a program and treatment providers makes case management all but impossible. It may be noted that in the case of UST, a program that did not utilize case management, the relationship between the EAP and care provider proved successful. 2. The program must have a highly trained staff that is prepared to deal with the problems and complex issues often associated with substance abuse treatment. A staff that is providing EAP/CM services should be licensed or be in position to be licensed in that particular state. Earlier the fact that diagnoses were often made far from the employee's residence was mentioned. 3. An EAP using the EAP/CM concept should have the ability to provide on-site services and not conduct business over the telephone. A possible boost to the bottom line is the availability of on-site EAPs to conduct workshops and training as well as preventative seminars. The program staff can also monitor the quality of treatment and the fees. 4. The program professionals must keep in mind that the core of the services lie in the ability to maintain assessment and sources of referral. The program may provide 8 to 10 sessions. This is cost savings but the staff must be wary. The cost could be lost if the patient has to be handed off to treatment beyond the scope of short term treatment. The process is lengthened with the hand over and time is lost in building a new trusting relationship with the new treatment provider.

Once the integration of EAP and Case Management takes place the system should provide structure in the EAP. The services will be conducted within the confines of the employee residential area. There will be a centralized location with the capability of providing consultation along with program coordination. The offices will be staffed with professionals with experience in dealing with the history of psychological as well as substance abuse problems. There will be a face-to-face evaluation prior to treatment recommendation and treatment recommendation can be made with a great deal of immediacy. The initial session with the provider can be scheduled within 48 hours. Preauthorization will be required. As the integration increases, the EAP can serve as in the capacity of negotiator for decreased fees for treatment that is in line with treatment length. Treatment is reviewed on a scheduled basis. Since the service is conducted in the residential area of the employee, the case manager is able to monitor both inpatient and outpatient resources. The case management system is afforded the opportunity for hands on involvement with the treatment community. The program personnel can update the treatment network. This gives the program the ability to uncover which facilities are providing the best treatment for the least cost. The program has the where-with-all to work with supervisors to identify and intervene with a troubled employee. The over all philosophy of an integrated system could save the organization a great deal of money. Unnecessary hospitalizations can be reduced and replaced with outpatient treatment, if appropriate. A local network base, providing high quality care at cost-efficient rates can be achieved.

An example of the effectiveness of the integration of EAP and Case Management is indicated by looking at Company A. The total health insurance for their 1000 employees was $1 million. The implementation of the integrated service cost $33,000. At the end on one year the cost of health insurance dropped to $500,000. Allowing for hidden costs of $50,000 and the $33,000 for the program, Company A gained a profit of $417,000 through the net savings on health insurance costs (Stanley, et al., 1988, pp., 229-241).

EDS Corporation and Case Management

EDS provides substance abuse and mental health care for their 53,000 employees. Those employees in need of assistance contact a therapist at the external EAP, where 12 counseling sessions are allowed. Of all the cases handled by the EAP almost 80% do not require further referrals. If more assistance is needed, the EDS case manager becomes involved. The case managers are all reported to be master's level clinicians with experience in the mental health and substance abuse fields and they oversee all chemical dependency and mental health treatment. The case manager asks the EAP to recommend the best local day treatment program or hospital. At this juncture, the case manager negotiates a rate. Authorization for the initial hospitalization is usually for 3 or 4 days. The case manager reviews the case and continues to review on an ongoing basis. This is meant to insure the proper treatment and appropriate setting for the employee. EDS saves money by providing the best service at an effective cost. By utilizing case management with it's EAP, EDS estimates savings at 40% to 50% over past expenditures before hospital negotiations. The process works differently in the EDS plant in the Dallas, Texas area. Accessing treatment is done in the same manner, including the 12 counseling sessions. If a referral is needed, the managed care company makes the referral through its network of approximately 50 providers. The Dallas study is incomplete. The completed study is geared toward measuring the progress of patients in therapy. Tracking session attendance as well as reduction in symptoms will be part of the report. In the final study, this information along with utilization reviews, number of out patient sessions, hospital admissions, length of hospitalization, rates and admissions per thousand will be analyzed. This information should show not only the quality of the treatment but the cost effectiveness. Meanwhile, EDS has already appreciated savings. Despite the increase in employees over the past two years, the dollar figure spent on mental health care has decreased. Metroplex PsychNetwork Inc., the provider group, has achieved savings of 30% in the treatment of mental health and substance abuse (Pine, 1994, p. 49 [2]).

Savings by self-insured unions through Case Management

Many labor local unions are self insured. Rates paid to inpatient and outpatient providers often come from a fund set up for that purpose. The Case Management technique, as applied by Michael W. Popp, Ph. D., Certified Addiction Counselor, show how effectively managing cases can lead to saving for the unions. Dr. Popp, a member of the Labor Assistance Professionals, is the Director of the Lower Hudson Valley Building and Construction Trades EAP, located in upper Westchester County, NY. The services provided by this organization have recently been expanded to cover local unions in New Jersey. His program is not connected with any health care company or treatment provider. He is autonomous and chooses from all available community resources capable of providing quality services. The staff is qualified, trained, and licensed. He uses face-to-face meetings with clients for the purpose of evaluations. He and his staff provide educational seminars and training to supervisory personnel. The Construction Trade EAP continuously monitors the facilities and constantly negotiates for the best service for the fewest dollars.

Dr. Popp has many agreements with a great deal of providers. Most of the agreements save the payor, in this case the union, a great deal of money. In subtracting the rate for services paid from the union fund from the rate posted by the service provider, we see the savings. In the most recent report to the Board of Directors of the Construction Trade EAP, Dr. Popp shows savings ranging from more than $15,000 to a savings of slightly under $1500 (Personal Communication, Feb. 1998). The Lower Hudson Valley Building & Construction Trades EAP provides an opportunity to view how unions save and at the same time retain complete confidentiality.

Now multiply the dollar savings to local unions accomplished by Dr. Popp by the number of Certified Labor Assistance Professionals. A unified front of Certified Professionals from the ranks of Organized Labor presents a potent bargaining chip when dealing with treatment providers, in-patient or out-patient. This keeps the cost of treatment down and allows communication between the local unions to determine just which facility has the best treatment for the least amount of money. It allows the smaller local unions, generating fewer patients, access to the same treatment at the same cost as the larger unions which traditionally received a lower rate because of the volume of patients. We now have Union Professionals not only making referrals but managing care and managing costs while maintaining and monitoring proper treatment. The shift from the traditional peer referral beginnings of Labor Assistance to the Professional approach by Labor People without losing the labor hands on, confidential peer approach will be examined.

Evaluation.

Another way of curtailing costs of providing assistance programs is to evaluate them on a fairly consistent basis. Times change and people change. Programs will also change. We have seen the diversity in programs. The assistance field has gone from a basic alcohol program to one that includes handling a wide range of problems. That range is ever broadening, getting bigger as time passes. We know there is no cookie cutter approach. If there is adherence to that belief, then programs need to be evaluated, each on its' own merits or faults.

If one believes the previous statement then my all time favorite saying that "liars figure and figures lie", comes into play. We can see the potential for problems in justifying ones position for programs as well as in statistics compiled. Both those for and against programs and those with an agenda to skew the real numbers could possibly make figures fit their views. There should be a mechanism or mechanisms for validating either position. The issue takes a slightly different bent from do they work to why do they work, and who needs help? This question should be why an almost complete generation, is not counted in many of the surveys complied on workplace alcohol and drug statistics"? We know people are retiring at an earlier age but to ignore the potential of an additional 15 year employee range is, from my perspective, irresponsible and a cover up.

Despite program success rates, some purported to be as high an 85%, there has been a lack of direction into investigating why they work. Reasons for this lack of investigation could be a combination of several issues or one single issue. There may be a lack of money or personnel who can evaluate a program; scientific instruments for the purpose of program evaluation may be missing; the organization may not care to evaluate their program; or as simple as not having planned the evaluation. In order to properly evaluate a program, several components should be in place.

Evaluation components

There needs to be commitment by all parties involved to conduct and support an evaluation. The source for causing an evaluation could be the union, the board of directors, managers or, the EAP people themselves. The cause does not have to be internal; it could come from the outside from groups such as the people funding the program or other organizations. The question of why, when and how the evaluation was conducted need to be answered.

Why an evaluation is conducted could be as simple as being told to do so or being politically correct within the organization. The reason is not as important as the need for honesty and cooperation between the program personnel and the organization. The why influences the when and how. When an evaluation should be conducted is sensitive. It appears to be beneficial to a program to have the evaluation early. This could aid in setting a baseline for comparison and address the issue of confidentiality. A long time period between inception and evaluation has problems. Staff has turned over and information has been lost. The program history may become muddled and the tracking of clients may be a problem. The how should be left up to those who know how to conduct an evaluation. Program personnel and managers should defer to those with the expertise and work with those experts.

The specification of goals and objectives need to be clearly understood. This, too, should be left up to the experts. The concept of the program must be placed in measurable and reachable terms. This includes time frames. What has and what will occur over a period of time. It also includes quantifiable data, which can be measured by services delivered and the outcome of those services.

Richard L. Peck (1995) reports similar inquires into program satisfaction, similar to the inquiries made in the Seagram program, are recommended. He interviewed Dr. John Bunker, ScD., MHS, a health care consultant for the largest independent human resources consulting firm in the world, The Wyatt Company. Dr. Bunker suggests that questions on the success of a program go beyond utilization data. He feels that satisfaction by a program user is of value. The company providing mental health and substance abuse assistance should know how the recipient of the treatment feels about the program. What was the quality of care? Were you listened to? How long did it take to get an appointment? In general, how do you feel about the program?

The information must be retrievable. On the surface, this may appear simple. That is not always true. Many organizations perceive themselves as having more than enough data when they are actually short on information. Many organizations have too much information about the employee and not enough pertaining to services offered and accepted (Holosko, 1988, pp. 59-66).

When it comes to evaluating treatment facilities, in my opinion, one of the truest forms of evaluation lies in examining the commitment of the facility to providing quality treatment. When you buy a car or a new electrical appliance, you usually get some kind of a warranty or guaranty. I get that with several of the treatment facilities I use. They show me that they are committed to providing the finest in treatment by committing to treating a relapsed patient, if that patient relapses before the end of 6 months from the date of discharge. There are caveats. The patient must have completed the treatment. They must have participated in treatment. Just sitting against a wall and not cooperating with counseling, either on an individual or group surrounding does not get it done. The patient must work toward being clean and sober. If that happens and that person relapses, they will be treated, in patient, free of charge. The EAP and MAP must know the facility and have knowledge of the staff. You can not buy a pig-in-a-poke when dealing lives. Treatment facilities do not want to take people back without being paid. This is an indicator that they provide good treatment. It could be very easy for some facilities to insist the patient complied with treatment recommendation and participated, actively, in treatment. That may not be true. It is incumbent on the EAP or MAP to stay on top of treatment and to use only facilities that provide quality assistance. They should be an integral part of the treatment team. Visiting facilities is recommended and periodic unscheduled visits are also recommended. Just having lunch with the marketing person does not constitute visiting a facility.

Regardless off who does the evaluation one thing remains clear. Treatment is a positive investment. The days of 28 impatient days are gone. The history of the 28 day stay is muddled. Some Insurance companies would pay for 28 some a little longer. In the new age of managed cost, since care is not managed but replaced by managed dollars, the 28 days is a thing of the past despite the figures produced by Scanlon that the longer the patient remains in patient, the better the chances for full recovery and less relapse. Even the Insurance Industry, the ones who created the 28 days stay find impatient treatment to be cost effective.

Blue Cross Blue Shield found that family care costs dropped by 87% after in-patient treatment. The difference? From $100 per month to $13.34 per month after 5 years. This same report from Substance Abuse in Brief, also shows Aetna Federal Employee Health overall health care costs of alcoholics of alcoholics rose from $130 to $1370 per month prior to treatment. Three years after treatment the medical cost for the same person drops to $190 per month.

Relapse

Since I mentioned relapse, I will give my thoughts on it. I personally do not believe in relapses. I believe they are a planned occasions. A person who has completed treatment, any kind of treatment, inclusive of AA is aware of the need to find a sponsor, to make meetings, make phone calls, take things one day at a time or even one minute at a time. They are taught to think things through. They are taught there are alternatives to drinking or drugging. The picking up the alcohol or drug is the final phase in relapse. The relapse began long before the actual substance use took place. No one ever said that remaining drug and alcohol was easy. What they do tell us is that it is simple. We tend to complicate things. That appears to be part of our make up. AA tells us to "Keep It Simple Stupid" (KISS). Just follow the suggestions and do not ask why. After a while the why becomes obvious. I have asked every person who relapsed if they called their sponsor before picking up the substance. The answer is a resounding 100% NO. The same answer and percentage applies to questions about going to meetings or making a call to another person in recovery. Relapses are planned. I know this will raise eyebrows and will cause argumentative conversations. This is my opinion. I do ask those who disagree with this opinion to ask individuals who relapsed the questions I suggest. The responses will be astounding. They may not be 100% but they will be in the very high nineties. Understand that I am all for treating a person who has relapsed. There treatment needs to include a strong focus on doing what needs to be done to prevent a recurrence of this problem.

<u>Summary</u>

We have now looked at different types of treatment. We find there is still help for free in Alcoholics Anonymous and there is the kind that can be paid for. We see that there are several treatment options available. They range from inpatient hospitalization to treatment allowing the person to attend meetings and treatment sessions on an out-patient basis. The history of medical benefits was discussed along with looking at how different people in different times viewed the problem of the alcoholic. Treatment for substance abuse and mental health is quite expensive and rising. There are ways of reducing costs or at least holding the line. Case Management and Utilization Reviews are methods of seeing the proper treatment is given for the correct amount of time required. Case management was responsible, in the example cited earlier, was responsible for an overall savings of over $400,000. The days of the automatic 28 day stay in rehabilitation facilities are gone. Other methods such as the one used by Dr. Popp are useful. He negotiates the price of treatment. While Dr. Popp is successful in his own right at negotiating his own rate, so is LAP. The thought of a consortium of Labor Assistance Programs using select facilities dramatically increases their power of negotiating an even better price than an individual, having a positive impact on the benefit dollar.

Evaluating the programs is also a method of curtailing costs. The ways of conducting an evaluation should be left to those who are familiar with programs. The goals and objectives of the evaluation must be clearly spelled out. The information must then be made readily available. The commitment of treatment and facilities is the real issue. It is recommended, wherever possible, that the EAPs and MAPs try and get some kind of guarantee for persons who successfully complete treatment and have subsequently relapsed. My own opinion or relapse not withstanding, relapse is real and needs to be addressed.

CHAPTER 8

We tend to look at the future as a long way off. The future is now. I like to relate the future to the past and see just how much time has passed. Think about this. By the time you see the next word and that word registers in your mind, that word and every word from here on in is in the past. It is history. If history can be so close, so can the future. We may live in the moment but by the time we realize, it is history. The future is the same. It is very close, as close as our next breath or blinking of an eye. We have to live in that ever so close future. We need to bring our ideas from the distant and very recent past and put them in the future. We need to update them and keep on improving what we have already accomplished. I am sure there could be an argument to do away with helping the substance abuser or mental health patient in the future but from what we have already seen, that may not be a good idea. EAPs and MAPs need to adapt to the changing times and changing ways. There will be a need for assistance programs. We will see what they need to do to survive and grow. We will look at managed care and how assistance programs are working with the new insurance. There will also be mentioned, new problems encountered by employees and members alike and how the EAPs and MAPs have taken steps to help.

EAPs and MAPs in the future

We have seen the past history of substance abuse and mental health and their relationship to the workplace of the past and present. We have seen how EAPs and MAPs began and evolved into the successful programs that they are. We have seen that they perform a service that is both necessary and cost efficient. There will be a place for them in the future. They will have to continue making adjustments as important and as innovative as making Labor Assistance Programs and the people charged with maintaining these programs more Professional.

They evolved from 19th century unionists helping their brothers and their families into corporate based programs. They have gone from peer pressure groups to sophisticated techniques. The common denominator is still the same. People. In order to serve the people in the future, certain changes will have to be made. EAPs and MAPs have to keep up with the changing times.

Previously, we saw assistance programs using utilization review and case management as methods for getting a handle on the problem of holding the line on escalating treatment costs. Dr. Popp is not the only one who negotiates fees for services with various treatment facilities. Many labor organizations are self insured. It is beneficial for them to make the best deal possible. It is their money. Always, they keep the welfare of the member in the forefront. I am not trying to infer that companies that do not have represented employees care any less than union represented employees. As we have seen, they have a different reason for achieving the same results. This evolutionary process has been going on for many years. It can not stop. If programs continue to adapt to the changing times, they will succeed. If they do not, they will fall by the wayside. The changes they made are not enough. They must continue changing.

<u>Is there a place for successful programs in the future?</u>

We have seen that there was and is a need for workplace assistance programs. We also see they will be needed in the future. The issue at hand is if employee and member assistance programs are successful, do they need to change? If there is a need to change, why is that necessary? What types of changes are necessary to keep these programs a viable part of the workplace of the future?

Change.

The cost of mental health care, inclusive of substance abuse treatment has risen dramatically. The hospitalization of patients for substance abuse and mental health problems has risen while hospitalization rate for other illnesses has dropped. The CNA Insurance company study revealed that the rate of admission for inpatient mental health and substance abuse treatment rose 25% between 1985 and 1987. The study also found that substance abuse and mental health treatment cost, per patient, was twice the cost of surgery, per patient. Earlier in this study the Foster Higgins survey was cited regarding the cost increases in treating substance abuse and mental health. Some of the reasons for the increase in the number of people getting help is the fact that there is an increase in benefits that cover chemical dependency and mental health problems. The stigma often attached to mental health has decreased. Lifestyles have become increasingly more stressful. It is estimated that 18.7% of Americans over the age of 18 have some kind of psychiatric disorder (Scanlon, 1991, pp. 54-55). Goff & Young (1996) report treatment costs of $12 billion being spent annually on depression. Gemignani (1996) tells us that depression costs corporate America $44 billion a year. Fifty-five percent of that amount is attributed to absenteeism and lost productivity. The American Medical Association is cited saying that 25% to 40% of patients treated in general hospitals are being treated for complications related to drinking. These problems appear in the areas of gastrointestinal, cardiovascular and reproductive disorders. The Institute of Medicine is cited saying substance abuse treatment has become one of the fastest growing and most expensive areas of health care in the 1980s. The increases generated huge profits for those in the industry. The National Institute on Alcohol Abuse and Alcoholism is cited as saying that despite the growth in the substance abuse treatment industry approximately 18 million Americans have problems related to the consumption of alcohol.

Profit associated with treatment cost.

    Treatment is expensive. The cost for inpatient treatment as
stated by Scanlon (1991) can range from $5,000 to $30,000 for
a twenty eight day stay in a rehabilitation facility. To show the
profit appreciated by inpatient treatment centers, he calculates
figures based on a 120 bed facility, billing at the rate of $350 a
day. If the facility had 36 patients and was reimbursed at 80%
of the $350 and figuring operating costs at $1,000 a day, there
would be a profit of $80 a day. If the facility was operating at a
full census and the payment was consistent, the facility would
realize a profit of $18,600 daily. This includes an allowance of
$15,000 a day for operating expenses. This breaks out to a profit
of 124%. If another $3,000 was allowed for marketing expenses,
the profit would drop to 87%. With profits like these, there is
little wonder as to why there is expansion and competition in
the field of chemical abuse treatment (Scanlon, 1991, pp. 89-90).
There is a facility in New York City that can only be described
as an ultra-private facility. They have a gourmet chef instead of
hospital cooks. They have music while relaxing. They even have
a high tea. This facility is affiliated with Columbia Presbyterian
Hospital. The rate is well over $2,500 a day. Insurance is not
accepted here. The actuality of it is someone has to pay.

    The bottom line comes into play again. The cost of care
is continuing to rise rapidly. The cost of mental health care
and substance abuse rehabilitation is growing. Competition
is increasing. The need for care is also growing. Assistance
programs seem to be effective. The numbers show there is a
return on investing in the rehabilitation of an employee. Health
care premium payors, usually the employer and insurance
companies are looking to change the paradigm for mental
health and substance abuse treatment. What companies want
to know is how to get the same quality of assistance for their
employees at a reduced cost. They also need to know if it can
be accomplished. That question may have an answer in the
managed care approach and by increased professionalism of

those in the assistance field. Evaluating programs could be of enormous value in retaining the proper program.

Managed care.

What is managed care? Managed care has been described as a product of insurance companies that attempt to balance the cost of services while continuing to provide quality care. It uses benefit incentives that are designed to eliminate or minimize unnecessary health care provider services. The objective of reducing health care benefit expenditures is achieved through the utilization of cost-containment measures such as case reviewing prior to hospital admission (precertification). Second surgical opinions, use of outpatient services as an alternative to inpatient care, and concurrent case review are other tools of managed care (Scanlon, 1991, p. 55). Richard T. Hellan, President, Personal Performance Consultants, Inc., of St. Louis, MO, describes managed health care:

> With respect to mental health and chemical dependence services, managed care is a systematic attempt to contain the rising costs of treatment through the development of employer-based programs that encourage prevention, and the coordination and administration of treatment accorded to individuals and groups (Simms, 1988, p. 33).

The Scanlon definition seems to encompass the entirety of health coverage while the definition of Richard Hellan as reported by Simms covers the mental health area. Hellan describes what managed care is trying to do. Ron Holman, Ph.D., President of the Holman Group of Canoga Park, California describes why managed care is concerned with mental health costs and the changes implemented to bring the costs under control.

> The Holman Group's view of the managed care stems from the frustration that resulted from doing what we call "old line" EAP, which allows individuals to check into a hospital or use the benefits packages at their discretion, exhaust

their lifetime benefits, and then come back to the EAP looking for some sort of help. Seeing this happen repeatedly over the course of time brought us to the point where, in the early 1980s, we started combining an EAP with a preauthorization hospital review that included a change in the benefit plan design.

The altered plan allows for the definition of medical necessity so that the length of hospital stay averages about eight days per admission, and the rest of the benefits dollars are spent on a variety of treatment modalities, including partial hospitalization, residential care, group homes, and day treatment programs (Simms, 1988, p. 34).

Some of the methods employed by managed care to reduce costs are establishing an annual dollar limit allocated for treatment services, establishing a preferred provider network or contracting with a health maintenance organization (HMO). Another part of the cost containment task is the use of physicians as gatekeepers (Scanlon, 1991, p. 55). A preferred provider network is composed of physicians and other professionals who are committed to accepting a set fee for their services. A gatekeeper is a person who is authorized to direct patients to what the gatekeeper feels is appropriate treatment. A particular problem with the gatekeeper process is that the gatekeeper is quite often not a physician. They can be Nurses, Social Workers, substance abuse counselors, or other mental health professionals. There is little and often no physical contact between the gatekeeper and the prospective patient. Recommendations for treatment are often based on one telephone conversation without the utilization of an assessment process or tool.

Scanlon (1991) does a fine job in describing the working of a gatekeeper or managed care reviewer. He feels that if a proper assessment is made by an EAP or treatment program professional, and that inpatient recommendation is viewed as the least restrictive method of treatment, the reviewer will likely concur. He also admits that the gatekeeper or reviewer can be many miles away. Concurrence is not necessarily true.

Scanlon (1991) states that one of the primary objectives of managed care is "care" not "cost." He also feels that the reviewer is professionally qualified and that the reviewer is utilizing accepted treatment standards. That is not always the case. If we recall that initially, gatekeepers were supposed to be physicians, we can see the beginning of failure. It is much cheaper to have a clerk or another person, who is not a physician handling the gatekeeper chores. When that gatekeeper is the insurance company or a company contracted by the insurance company to do gatekeeper work, we see where there could be a conflict.

A report on Managed Behavioral Health Care Services presented to The Congressional Budget Office reveals some alarming shortcomings in the way managed care handles substance abuse treatment. The problem lies in the restrictions placed by managed care on admission for in-patient or intensive out-patient treatment of chemical dependency. Some of the requirements are limiting the benefit to substance abusers who have a general medical condition such as high blood pressure. Persons with personality disorders are excluded. Failing treatment for chemical dependency at a lower level of treatment prior is a prerequisite for admission to a higher level of treatment. A person is required to attempt harming him or herself within the previous 24 hours or take significant action to harm another person within the past 24 hours or threaten action to damage property with a high degree of lethality. Many experts in the chemical dependency field feel a person should be placed in a detoxification facility to prevent delirium tremors (D. Ts.). They feel that intoxication with signs of withdrawal indicates a need for detoxification services. The managed care requirement for admission to detoxification was a diagnostically confirmed addiction with indications of D. Ts. This requirement appears to put the patient in harms way. The author of that report conducted an in-depth review of the charts maintained by case managers. The review disclosed significant clinical problems in both the diagnostic and referral areas. The range of problems ran from 30% to 58%. In cases of substance use disorders or cases where strong indications of substance use disorders were present, there were problems in 54.8% to 78.3%. The failure rate in not properly diagnosing and evaluating substance abuse and addiction was 21.9% to 31.3% (Wrich, Sept. 1996). The bottom line is visited again. For a managed care company to prove success, it must show savings while continuing to provide quality care. We have seen that providing the quality care is not always the case. Failing that, it is quite possible a new managed care company may succeed in convincing the payor that theirs' is a better approach.

There is a real danger in the way some managed care companies look at treating substance abusers. In my opinion, the piece involving accessing a less intrusive mode of assistance, i.e., out-patient treatment prior to being considered for in-patient treatment is an absurdity. I have had conversations with gatekeepers where they told me that the person I was trying to place in a rehabilitation facility had to try out-patient treatment and *fail* before that person could be admitted to an in-patient facility. Anyone who works with substance abusers know that getting the person to realize they have a problem is one of the most difficult parts or getting someone the help they need. The denial is strong and often bolstered by the support of family members, friends, the employer, fellow union members, and fellow employees. When the abuser makes that all important breakthrough, the last thing he or she needs is someone telling them that their problem is not that bad. That is what happens when someone is finally convinced they have a problem and the insurance company says your problem is not severe enough for you to be hospitalized. Most alcoholics and drug addicts do not want to hear how bad their problem is. When they admit it is bad, they believe they need help. They find it easy to view out-patient treatment as a way of someone telling them that their problem is *not that bad.* I view that as giving them a chance at another drinking or drugging episode.

I am not advocating the old ways of instant rehabilitation for 28 days. What I am advocating is a better method of problem identification and intensity. The gatekeeper, as we have seen earlier, is removed entirely for any contact with the potential patient. The gatekeeper gets paid to see that the patient gets the best, most appropriate, and cost efficient treatment possible. Without a proper diagnosis this becomes little more than a guessing game. EAPs and MAPs have physical contact with the patient. The gatekeeper does not. Often, the EAP and the MAP have prior personal knowledge of the individual, the intensity of the problem, and the length of time involved. The gatekeeper does not. The EAP and the MAP often have attendance and work performance records available. The gatekeeper does not. Some EAPs and MAPs use assessment and valuation tools. The gate keeper does not. All in all the advantage of knowing the breadth and depth of the problem seems to lie with the assistance professionals. It stands to reason the assistance people would have a better understanding of the needs of the client or patient. EAPs and MAPs often recommend outpatient treatment as appropriate treatment. This begs the question as to why managed care does not challenge assistance professionals when they recommend out-patient treatment over in-patient treatment.

When looking at the Brief Summary of Audit Findings of Managed Behavioral Health Care Services submitted to The Congressional Budget Office, presented in Sept. 1996, we see what I believe to be a failure in providing necessary services. Bruce Vladeck, Administrator, Health Care Financing Administration in Washington, DC, participated, via telephone, in a conference on managed care. The conference was held at the Harvard Club in New York City on Dec. 5, 1996. In his remarks he said,

> "...In much of the country the managed care plans are succeeding, at least for the time being, in an effort that neither government nor private purchasers were able to carry out earlier, and that is, basically, reduce what they pay to the providers of service" (A Breakfast Conversation with Government, Banking, Health and Religious Leaders, Dec. 5, 1996, p.4).

His findings come on the heels of the Brief Summary of Audit Findings of Managed Behavioral Health Care Services submitted to The Congressional Budget Office, 1996. We have to ask ourselves if this is proof that patients are suffering at the hands of the profiteers. We know that, in the past, EAPs and MAPs almost had carte blanche in referring a patient to treatment. All too often 28 days for rehabilitation coupled with 3 to 7 days for detoxification was almost automatic. For years, the insurance industry paid, with little complaint. Assistance professionals were not challenged in their recommendation of treatment until fairly recently. Granted, not every patient required that type or length of treatment. It looks as if the pendulum has swung the other way. Ask any EAP or MAP if they feel they are getting the proper treatment for their patients or clients. Most of them will tell you that in cases where they truly feel inpatient treatment for 21 days or longer is necessary, they can not get approval for such treatment from the insurers. Combine this with Scanlon's findings that the longer the stay the better and we see a failing system.

Outpatient treatment is less costly than inpatient treatment. It appears to make sense to utilize outpatient facilities, if that particular treatment is properly recommended. Implying that managed care categorically refuses to allow all inpatient treatment is both unfair and untrue. The problem may lie in "teaching old dogs new tricks'. We have seen the cost of treatment escalate. Profits in the treatment industry are astronomical. Competition is growing. Insurance companies want to get a grip on the escalating costs and payors do not want to see their premiums rising. However, the insurance industry seems to be rephrasing the "old dogs" adage into "kicking the old dogs and no new tricks". Labor also has an interest in lowering the cost of insurance. The employee/member, on the surface, appears to be the recipient of health care benefits at no cost. This is not true. The employee/member is paying for the insurance. Money allocated for insurance premiums is part of the overall financial package brought to the bargaining table by management. Money not spent on insurance could easily wind up in the paycheck. As salary rise so do union dues. Labor wants to see that the member gets help. Organized labor wants to hang on the benefits that they have bargained for over the past decades. Management and labor want the individual to get help. Often, in the past, a program representative needed only to pick up the phone and have someone admitted to rehabilitation for 28 days. Insurance paid. The program personnel did their job, the insurance company did its' job, and the employee or member went away for a month. If we go back to Dr. Holman, we may see the problem. Benefit exhaustion and still a need for assistance.

There was a need for a better method of determining the type and length of treatment. The professionalism of program personnel began to come under scrutiny. There were rumors of sweetheart deals between referrers and 28 day programs. People in charge of programs had not shown the desire or ability of using assessment tools in selecting proper treatment for a particular problem. Things had to change.

EAPs & MAPs; growth in professionalism and expansion of problems.

> As health care in America evolves into a managed care environment, certified alcohol counselors and other EAP practitioners will be likely to gravitate to more comprehensive programs than EAPs. Their role and expertise will remain unmatched by other professional. Nonetheless, they will find that EAPs will become components of a greater system rather than separate, unintegrated, and uncontrolled parties in the health care puzzle. The evolution is occurring now and will be complete over the course of the next decade...(Lee, 1988, p. 75).

The decade of evolution has yet to pass and we have already seen major changes in the field of assistance programs. They have not only become more professional, they have policed themselves and instituted certification. Previously we saw that ALMACA evolved into the Employee Assistance Professionals

Association (EAPA). Any one in the EAP-MAP field, if they choose, can be a member of EAPA but not every EAPA member can be a Certified Employee Assistance Professional (CEAP). To get to the plateau of certification, a test created, given, supervised, and graded by EAPA must be taken and passed. The test consists of 250 questions. The allotted time is 4 hours. Two years experience in the assistance field is required before testing eligibility. Credentialing increases annually. In 1996 there were approximately 6240 CEAPs. In 1997 there was an increase of well over 1000, bringing the number of CEAPs to approximately 7500. Another acknowledgment to the increased professionalism of assistance professionals is indicated in the other professional titles held by CEAPs. These titles encompass a myriad of professions from Marriage and Family Counselors to Doctors of Theology, from Social Workers to Doctors of Philosophy, from MDs. to Masters of Public Health and all manner of addiction specialists and counselors. Not only was there a distinct need for expansion of services, there was a change in what was happening. It appears that the broad brush may be getting broader.

The road to increased professionalism was not a walk in the park. By the time the late 1960s rolled around there were plenty of people around who knew about alcohol problems and the workplace. Many had years of experience but there was no solid organization or coalition. There were movements in the areas of establishing federal organizations and state alcoholism directors. In 1970 the Hughes Act (Comprehensive Alcohol Abuse and Alcoholism Prevention, Treatment, and Rehabilitation Act) caused the formation of the NIAAA, which established the Occupational Programs Branch. This group was responsible for getting the support to address workplace alcoholism. Workplace programs throughout the country became a supplier of occupational programs consultants for NIAAA. Thirty individuals referred to as the "Dirty Thirty were recruited to assist. When consultants or mentors were needed in assisting workplace alcohol issues, the consultant closest to the point of need was assigned. When NIAAA allocated

$50,000 to each state for three years, beginning in 1972, for the purpose of hiring two consultants, one in the private and the other in the public sector, the "Dirty Thirty" expanded to the "Thunderin' Hundred". In 1974 the then Joint Commission on Accreditation and Healthcare (JCAH), now the Joint Commission on Accreditation and Healthcare organizations (JCAHO), recommended to NIAAA that program personnel be certified. Little was done at that time and eventually, in the mid 1980s, credentialing of EAPs came under the jurisdiction of the Employee Assistance Certification Commission (EACC) of the EAPA. EAPA was formerly known as ALMACA. ALMACA was formed in April of 1971 and changed the name to EAPA in 1989 (Bickerton, 1990).

EAPA keeps educating the membership. After becoming a Certified Employee Assistance Professional the credentials must be renewed every 3 years. This is not automatic. EAPA has monthly meetings. At these meeting, training is given. Topics include EAP Supervision, The Future of MAPs in a Managed Care Environment, Mastering Stress, Women and Work, and many other subjects. Two Professional Development Hours are given for attending the training. A total of 60 Professional Development Hours is required for renewal. Without proof of at least 60 development hours the credential will not be renewed. In order to reestablish credentials after letting them lapse, the test must be taken and passed again. This way EAPA ensures its' members are kept up to date with new developments in the field of employee or member assistance.

I think it is important to not that, especially for Labor Professionals, it is not necessary to be an EAPA member to be a CEAP. Labor Assistance Professionals is just what it says, Labor Professionals. The increased professionalism of Labor Assistance Programs, developed and taught by qualified Labor Assistance Professionals will be discussed in the last chapter.

An overview of the growth will indicate two extremely important facts. Fact number one is there is a growth in the industry of assistance as well as expansion. No longer is the traditional approach to treating a person for chemical dependency completely viable. We have seen there are numerous persons who have a multiplicity of problems, stress and chemical dependency, bulimia and dependency, to name two. The second fact is as the problems become increasingly complex, there becomes the need for growth in the assistance programs and professionals. Ascertaining information that an individual is an alcoholic or drug abuser no longer means that the individual is handed over for the traditional 28 day rehabilitation. There is a need to determine if there are additional problems. If the answer is in the affirmative, then appropriate treatment needs to be prescribed. The assistance professional making a referral today needs to be able to recognize the complete problem at hand or at least recognize that the issue may not be a simple one of alcoholism or drug dependence. The patient needs to be matched to the appropriate treatment. This is how things are currently being done and will probably continue on for some time. Managed care doesn't always say no to inpatient treatment. What it often asks is weather the treatment recommended is appropriate. If EAPs and MAPs do not use the same tools or exercise similar expertise as the gatekeepers, there will be a continuing conflict between the person making the referral and the managed care company. The other side of this coin is that gatekeepers will no longer be able to deny recommended treatment out of hand without the fear of repercussion.

<u>What must these programs do to stay viable in the continuing evolution of managed care?</u>

To remain viable in the future, assistance programs will have to learn to deal with the managed care companies. There is no indication that managed care, in one shape or another, is going anywhere in the near future. No one is always right or wrong. The study looked at various tools that may offer an assistance program person an avenue of direction.

When making a recommendation for treatment, either inpatient or outpatient, it is important that as much knowledge about the individual as possible be available. A proper assessment is crucial to achieving that goal. One of the ways to relatively assure that the recommended treatment is appropriate is to match the individual to the proper treatment modality. This approach will, hopefully, be resultant of properly using assessment tools.

Professionalism is being sought after by the managed care companies regarding the recommendation of treatment. The study previously addressed the practice of placing an individual in treatment for 28 days. The old way was a one size fits all attitude. We have seen that this approach is no longer appropriate. The problems were rarely as simple as they appeared to be. If a person was heavy and drank to excess and was categorized as an alcoholic, the weight was often attributed to the alcohol. If a person was using cocaine, heroin, or other illegal drugs and was thin, the thinness was attributed to the use of drugs. Rarely was the weight looked at other than a residual effect of substance abuse. If a person was depressed, they drank to feel better. If they were nervous or hyper, they drank to calm themselves. Today we see that there is a relationship between behaviors and that they are often just as serious as the obvious addiction. It is doubtful that one illness can be treated and the other ignored while expecting success. Appropriate treatment needs to be identified and carried through. One patient with two illnesses still presents one patient. It does little or no good to treat half a patient.

When it comes to recognizing the problem or problems suffered by a union member or company employee, it is apparent the problem be recognized accurately and as early as possible. Equally important is getting proper, cost efficient treatment. There are several tools available that could enable proper assessment. Proper matching the problem with the patient is presented in Project MATCH (Matching Alcoholism Treatment to Client Heterogeneity: Project MATCH Post treatment Drinking Outcomes). Unfortunately, Project Match appears to come up short in matching.

The matching process is exclusionary. It does not include people who use other drugs and alcohol. There is a disproportionate number of men to women. Women are not fairly represented. People suffering from psychoses and those with organic illnesses were also excluded as were those who had little prospect for finding adequate housing. There was no mention of assessment or use of assessment tools. This begs the question as to how were the candidates selected? Also, there was no control group. As stated, there are several assessment tools available that could have possibly been utilized in screening possible study cases for Project MATCH.

In the world of managed care and dwindling health care dollars, it behooves assistance programs to assess and recommend proper treatment for those compounded or complicated illnesses. "In effective MAPs, clients are matched with treatment programs exactly suited to their mix of needs" (Bacharach, et al., 1994, p. 58). Matching makes sense. If a person is dual diagnosed with substance abuse and an eating disorder, the relationship between both problems has to be identified and worked on. One illness must be treated with the same interest as the other. Treatment selection is tremendously important. There are some substance abuse treatment people who believe the treatment approach to an eating disorder should be similar to the treatment of substance abuse. Mental health professionals that are experienced in dealing with disorders are known to have a history of under diagnosing substance abuse problems. They also do not properly medicate substance abusers. Many substance abusers distrust these people. They frequently turn to programs like O.A. The rewards for the cessation of substance abuse are more measurable and observed much earlier in recovery from substance abuse than from an eating disorder. This is but one example of the need for matching the patient to the proper treatment (Zweben, 1987, p. 189).

In order to provide possible solutions to the problems associated with achieving these goals, we should investigate some assessment tools. Some are old and some are more recent.

Assessment Tools

We have come to see the concerns of managed care companies and why payors are adopting the managed care plans. The payor wants the most for the dollar. Managed care is also managing costs. They want the best care for the least amount of money. We have seen why managed care has become as popular as it is. We have seen why certain groups have been reluctant to accept managed care. No one wants to be shown as incapable of doing their job. There is little doubt that any one would want their diagnosis or recommendation for treatment over ruled by a stranger many miles away. The stranger has, as stated previously, little or no contact with the client. If both the program personnel and the managed care company or gatekeeper were all on the same page at the same time, this problem might be alleviated. The key may be as simple as identifying the problem or problems properly, the first time.

Proper identification of any problem is extremely important. This importance takes on another dimension in evaluating or assessing the relationships of problems. Assistance programs and those who are providing treatment, should be aware that there are tools available that help assess a myriad of problems, not just chemical dependency. Two of the tools available are the Addiction Severity Assessment Program (ASAP) and Focus. The speed with which these tools can be used is enhanced by the use of computers. ASAP (Wallace, S. 1997) is completed by a counselor or therapist while the Focus (Gould) is completed by the patient. Both identify problems faced by the individual. Employee and member assistance personnel as well as providers should find that these tools facilitate a faster and more complete identification of a problem or issue than the traditional one-on-one or face-to-face intake or initial evaluation. They will also identify more than one problem, facilitating the recommendation of the proper treatment at the out set. These tools can not only identify problems but when used to their full capacities, can provide treatment plans. These tools seem to fit the needs of the EAP-MAP people as well as the managed care people. They provide two important elements that enhance treatment effectiveness. Speed and accuracy on one hand and time saving on the other hand. ASAP is a computerized version of the Addiction Severity Index (ASI). The ASI (Franzese) was developed in 1980 by A. T. McLellan. Franzese tells us that the ASI is successful in identifying problems other than chemical dependency. The ASAP not only identifies the problems by using the ASI format, it has been enhanced to provide treatment plans. The Focus provides the same basic information as the ASAP with one glaring distinction. The Focus program is self administered by the client or patient. Focus will not provide a treatment plan since it is basically an intake or assessment tool that has been extracted from another program known as Self Discovery. Self Discovery will be discussed shortly. The previously mentioned Dr. Roger Gould is the developer of Focus and Self Discovery, along with several other computerized mental health programs. Dr. Gould maintains that the Focus will provide data in one session that would normally take three to five sessions to extract. The Self Discovery program is 5 sessions in length. It helps identify and solve many problems, not just substance abuse problems. Ideally, a person should be able to work through the issues before reaching the fifth session. That plateau is used to help people work through issues that prevent them from achieving success within the first four steps. Dr. Gould has developed another innovative program dealing with stress. It is called Mastering Stress. It helps identify problems or a problem, helps to find a solution for the problem. If there is reticence on the part of the client to work on specific issues, the program has a third component that helps identify and remove those things that prevent getting help. Of course the program will recommend seeking professional services if they are necessary. If time is truly money, programs such as ASAP and Focus and relief provided by them could prove to be extremely valuable. They will help identify just what the problem is and what type of treatment is necessary. With Self Discovery and Mastering

Stress, treatment may not be necessary. The client may be able to work through the issues and solve the problems on his or her own with the help of these computerized programs.

Acupuncture

The ancient Chinese practice of acupuncture is being used in treatment of chemical dependency. It can be used in inpatient treatment, out patient treatment, or even be used in the offices of assistance personnel. It works and is relatively inexpensive. It has gained acceptance as shown by the number of insurance companies that pay on acupuncture treatment claims. Prudential, Metropolitan Life, John Hancock, Aetna life and Casualty, Liberty Mutual Insurance Companies, and Travelers insurance Companies are just some of the insurance companies that have been paying on acupuncture treatment (Mitchell, 1987, p. 98). Blue Cross Blue Shield has recently joined other major insurance companies in paying acupuncture treatment claims. Blue Cross has an insurance group named Blue Choice. One of the largest participating organizations in Blue Choice is AT&T. Recently Blue Choice announced it would pay for acupuncture done by in-network acupuncturists. When I questioned them about the network, they admitted they had none in place but would pay for acupuncture treatment provided by any licensed acupuncturist.

An important part of the auricular acupuncture treatment is detoxification.

> Acupuncture reduces the intensity of physical signs of withdrawal; stimulates the digestive system and other avenues of elimination, to rid the body of toxic wastes; and relieves depression and insomnia, which can last for a long time after detoxification and really undermine your willpower (Mitchell, 1987, p. 73).

Acupuncture will not solve the problem alone. Counseling is quite possibly necessary. Support systems such as A.A. and N.A. may be in order. One particular program that provides acupuncture and the ancillary programs necessary for treatment is in Lincoln Hospital in the South Bronx section of

New York City. The program is inexpensive. In 1987 the cost was less that $30 per treatment (Mitchell, 1987). The program is directed by Dr. Michael Smith, a physician, psychiatrist and acupuncturist, who is also the program developer. To become an auricular acupuncturist, one must receive 80 hours of training and supervised experience. This treatment is provided by Dr. Smith and his staff. The importance of this in relationship to EAPs and MAPs is in the area of cost saving. The training is free. Dr. Smith and his staff have trained thousands of people from all parts of the globe in auricular acupuncture. Just about any persons involved in chemical dependency treatment can gain acceptance to the Lincoln Hospital program. A medical degree or full acupuncture licensing is not necessary. There is a accreditation for auricular detoxification acupuncturist.

<u>Does acupuncture provide a benefit for the workplace?</u>

A study completed by the Kent/Essex Detox Center in Delaware provides some insight to the question (Anderson, June 1996). Based on their findings, it cost $6.71 per admission for those receiving acupuncture. With admission during the study at 878, the cost was $5,889. Those receiving acupuncture as part of the treatment were matched against a control group not using acupuncture. The study concluded that those who received acupuncture participated in treatment on a higher level than those who did not. The rate of persons leaving treatment against medical advice was lower for the acupuncture group. The acupuncture group had longer periods of sobriety than the other group. Upon completion of the study it was recommended that acupuncture treatment be offered at other sites. It was also recommended that acupuncture be made available to those in the community that have been discharged from detox programs. Another recommendation was the inclusion of the ASI and the purchase of computerized scoring package. This could be used to measure the success of the program while it was ongoing.

Adding acupuncture to treatment or to an assistance program, either a work program or union program is, is fairly simple. The training is free. No academic or medical degrees are required. It is covered by payment from many insurance companies. After being trained, a detoxification program can be set up. In New York State the program must be under the supervision of a licensed acupuncturist. The licensed acupuncturist will monitor the treatment and the progress. He or she signs off on the records regarding acupuncture. They do not necessarily have to be on site for treatment application but they are responsible.

There are other methods that could help reduce the cost of treating people. They could conceivably benefit all the parties involved in the process, assistance people, treatment people, traditional insurance companies, managed care companies. Most of all, the employee or member could possibly be the biggest beneficiary.

New payers in the game.

Compounding the problem of trying to keep costs down is the increase of areas in which EAPs and MAPs are getting involved. The broad brush is getting broader.

There are other reasons for a broad brush approach being adopted by all parties. There are several problems facing the workplace and thereby, affecting EAPs and MAPs. These problems differ on the surface. Beneath that surface there is, all too often, the common denominator of substance abuse. The more things seem to be different, the more they have in common. Substance abuse continues to be a major problem along with mental health. Today we are finding the substance abuse and stress problems are linked to and often rooted in other serious problems.

When I spoke of the number of women in treatment, one important reason for the problems of chemically dependent women was not mentioned. Many women in treatment for chemical dependency have been identified as being sexually abused as a child or and adult. This sexual abuse is inclusive of incest and rape. Often substance abuse is the end result of not being able to cope with the trauma and stress induced by these forms of assault. This is a tragic incident. It does, however, come to the attention of EAPs and MAPs. Today, more than 50% of the workforce is female.

Bulimic patients exhibit higher levels of impulsive behavior. The bulimic person will induce vomiting after eating as a method of keeping weight off or as a method of losing weight. This behavior translates into history of more suicide attempts, psychiatric hospitalizations, and more episodes of stealing. 82% of cocaine users who did not experience disorders reported on eating binges of twice a month or less. Those who could be categorized as bulimic reported binge eating of once a week. That rate was 60%. Cocaine is an appetite suppressant. People who abuse cocaine are often very thin. For this reason anorexics are drawn toward cocaine. An anorexic is a person who is obsessed with weight loss. They often starve themselves and exercise obsessively. They are never thin enough. Simply put cocaine makes anorexics not want to eat. Persons suffering from bulimia are often drawn toward heroin since heroin often induces vomiting.

There is a relationship between chemical dependency and mental health issues such as depression. Sternberg, (1989), reports that in a particular study group of 198 dual diagnosed patients, 37% of the group showed major depression while another 28% displayed bipolar spectrum disorders. Interestingly enough, the study indicated that cocaine addicts treated during the time of the study, suffering from bipolar spectrum disorders, used cocaine mostly when in a manic/hypnotic state. This may be caused by the desire to elevate to another mood. A bipolar person is one who moves from a manic state to a depressed state. Bipolar disorders can be referred to as manic-depression. The study showed that 21% to 39% of persons with a substance abuse problem met the criteria for other psychiatric disorders. Between 30% and 60% of substance abusers who have been hospitalized report significant depression symptoms. The study also showed that while euphoria may be a result of the use of heroin, cocaine and alcohol, chronic use of these drugs can lead to anxiety, belligerence and depression. Attention deficit was identified in 23% with an additional 21% being categorized as antisocial (Sternberg, 1989, pp. 71-72).

A great many assistance professionals are credentialed as alcohol counselors or substance abuse counselors. Employee and Member Assistance Professionals are not just dealing with alcoholics and drug addicts. When they come across a person who is suffering from multiple disorders, it would be in the best interest of all parties for the EAP or MAP to refer the client out to a specialist in the necessary field. Proper use of an assessment tool may help identify this type of problem or individual.

Assistance professionals were dealing with more complex issues than traditional alcohol and drug abuse problems. Depression, anxiety, and stress, are words program people were beginning to hear more frequently. AIDS was another new condition and problem that fell, in many cases, in the assistance area. One particular reason that assistance persons are getting involved is those infected with HIV are working and living longer. The Family and Medical Leave Act (FMLA) and the Americans with Disabilities Act (ADA) are pieces of legislation designed to help the worker. FMLA helps a worker deal with personal and family illnesses and issues. The ADA prohibits discrimination against those suffering from disabilities. Both these pieces of legislation require employers to make reasonable accommodations for employees with HIV/AIDS. If health benefits are provided by the employer or the union and HIV/AIDS coverage is specifically excluded, the exclusion should be challenged under the ADA (Einloth & Hauck, 1997, p 1).

AIDS is primarily a health issue but when a serious contributor to the spread of this infection is traced to the sharing of needles by intravenous drug users, the need for program participation in AIDS policies and programs becomes clear. Roman & Blum (1989) said that assistance people were being drawn into the forming of AIDS policies with a greater degree of frequency. Between 100 and 150 men, women and children are diagnosed with AIDS every 24 hours. It is the leading cause of death for men and women between the ages of 25 & 44. More than half of all working people fall into this age category. Half of all new HIV infections are occurring in people under the age of 25, the workforce of tomorrow.

There is a relationship between substance abuse and eating disorders. "Clinicians involved in substance abuse treatment have been aware for some time that women with alcohol and other drug abuse problems also frequently suffer from eating disorders" (Zweben, 1987, p. 181). More than one third of bulimic patients relate issues of alcohol and drug problems along with substantial social impairment. Bulimic sufferers induce vomiting as a method of keeping weight off. Heroin induces vomiting. An anorexic is a person who is obsessed with weight loss. They often starve themselves and exercise excessively. Many turn to cocaine since it is an appetite suppressant (Zweben, 1987, p. 182). The problem of an eating disorder is more complex than just drugs and eating or drugs and not eating. Bulimia and anorexia have a similarity in afflictions but a difference in age groups. The similarity lies in the illness. Both are dealing with weight problems. The difference is in the age group. A person suffering from bulimia is older than the anorexic. Their problem stems from difficulty for a family and an adolescent moving from adolescence into young adulthood and the independence that often accompany such a transition. The anorexic, on the other hand, has trouble with the family while moving from childhood into adolescence (Root, Fallon & Friedrich, 1986). Why is this now a problem for EAPs and MAPs? The young adult is in the workplace and the adolescent may be a dependent of an employee.

The complexity of the problem is expanded when we look at women in treatment. For the most part, mental health professionals are not trained in determining a substance abuse problem. This becomes more of a problem when the eating disorder is a substitution for a substance abuse problem. Those seeking help for eating disorders often report alcohol or other drug use in the past. However, at the time of treatment there does not appear to be any problems with substances. This presents a new challenge for the assistance professionals (Zweben, 1987).

Summary

Things have changed in the world of Employee and Member Assistance. If they stood their ground and dealt with only alcohol problems, as some assistance purist desired, they probably would have gone the way of the dinosaur. Union recognized, early on, that assistance needed to cover more than alcohol. They also realized that assistance should be offered to families of members.

If assistance programs have a place in the future, they will have to change their methods. No longer can assistance focus on substance abuse problems as a sole problem for workers and the workplace. Employers are recognizing what the unions recognized years before. You need to treat more than alcohol and you need to extend that help to the family, not just the employee.

Managed care made its presence felt. EAPs and MAPs found them difficult to deal with. Managed care was concerned with cutting the costs of medical and mental health benefits. On was they accomplished that feat was to put a tight rein in the on EAPs and MAPs in their ability to place clients and patients in treatment and rehabilitation. The gatekeepers of the insurance industry made it almost impossible for assistance professionals to access the treatment they felt was necessary. In an effort to increase the professionalism of assistance professionals and to give them a little more credibility with insurance companies and the gatekeepers, credentialing became more important. Today, EAPs and MAPs are not only credentialed as CEAPs, the ranks of CEAPs include Doctors, Theologians, Psychologist, Nurses, and many other professions. The Occupational Programming Consultants, who dealt almost exclusively with workplace alcohol problems, have grown into a profession with greater ability and more talent. The talent comes from a growing professional group along with the recovering peer group. Both are achieving a higher plain academically and clinically.

The newer and more effective method of getting treatment for a client or patient is to match that person with the treatment needed. One of the methods of ascertaining just what issues need to be addressed can be uncovered through the proper use of assessment tools. ASAP, ASI, and Focus are all assessment tools and are available today. Mastering Stress and Self-Discovery are programs that can help the individual identify and possibly solve issues of stress. Both programs are self-administered and both give a great deal of confidentiality. They can be used in conjunction with a mental health professional or they can be used on their own by the client. All of the computerized should make it easier for the professional to identify a multiplicity of problems, if they exist. If only one problem presents itself, so be it. Whether with a mental health professional or without these programs should help in two ways. They should help alleviate the problem and they are less costly than traditional mental health treatment. It should be *clearly* understood that these programs, be they assessment tools or problem solving tools, are not aimed at doing sway with mental health treatment or mental health practioniers. These programs help the mental health professional. They too are feeling the ax wielding of the managed care company. Proper utilization of these tools will allow the mental health professional to see more patients. The big difference is that they should get to the root of the problem in a quicker time period. In Focus alone, Dr. Gould believes the program will extract as much information from the patient that takes traditional methods 3 to 5 sessions.

We saw where illnesses that were not the normal problem encountered by EAPs and MAPs have become a concern for them. Eating disorders like bulimia and anorexia have gained notoriety. These disorders are gaining attention in the assistance field for various reasons. One is the broad brush approach and the other by stretching the traditional views of assistance programs. Bulimia and anorexia often have a strong relationship to chemical dependency. Depression is also a problem gaining more attention in the assistance field. Many persons hospitalized for depression have a past history of chemical dependency.

CHAPTER 9

For the most part EAPs and MAPs have handled just about anything tossed their way. They have always been ready to help. The future will be no different in helping. What and how they will help will change. They now deal with problems faced by members and employees, as well as their families, in the world of corporate downsizing or layoffs. Being laid off is an extremely traumatic experience for a worker used to receiving a check and benefits. The effects of a layoff can be devastating. Assistance people are in the midst of it all trying to make the transition less threatening and in some cases getting people back on the payroll. EAPs and MAPs are faced with dealing more and more with incidents of violence in the workplace.. They are gaining more exposure and acceptance in the world of small business. Previously, for the most part, EAPs were found in business employing large numbers of workers and MAPs were set up for union members and their families. We will see how the changes are coming about. Finally, we will see the impact of drug testing in the workplace and how it is being handled by both employee and union assistance personnel.

The Future of EAPs and MAPs Is Here

We have seen where EAPs and MAPs have come from and how they have grown. We also saw how they have changed with the times in an effort to continue their purpose. They have adjusted for the future in the past. They will have to continue to broaden their concept of helping individuals. The world of today offers new challenges. EAPs and MAPs have answered the call. They have been sought out by management to assist in ways that, until recently, were completely foreign to them. EAPs and MAPs are becoming more involved in handling the problems of employees facing layoffs and in assisting in getting sick and disabled employees and members back on the active workplace payroll. They are involved in working in the area of workplace violence. Where once EAPs and MAPs were the province of large businesses we are seeing a growth of assistance programs in small businesses. Another problem assistance programs are becoming familiar with is in dealing with workplace drug testing.

<u>Assistance Programs and Downsizing</u>

Downsizing is a word that is supposed to make the world comfortable. It sounds better than layoffs, which is exactly what downsizing is. We play with words to make the end result of what they mean appear more comfortable and less threatening. We no longer have used cars or used watches; we have previously owned cars and watches. Video stores, after successfully renting movies, sell them as previously viewed movies, not used tapes, which is what the actually are. We no longer have rain storms, we have rain events. The serious felony crime of robbery, forcibly removing property from a person, is reduced to purse snatching. Previously owned sounds better than buying a used piece of equipment. Sounds like someone owned the car or watch previously but never used it. Purse snatching does not sound as serious as robbery. Previously viewed sounds better than buying a tape or DVD that may have been put through a machine several hundred times. A rain event does not sound as threatening as a severe thunder storm. Downsizing sounds a lot better that lay off. It does not sound as harsh as lay off. Lay off has the double "f" sound in off. It sounds a lot harder than the softer "ing" in downsizing.

Management has found a new way of using their program personnel. Rohm & Haas is a special chemical company located in Philadelphia, PA. The EAP showed its value to the company by helping reduce long-term disabilities by from $1.2 million to approximately $108,000 in 1992. Now they are using their EAP for the purpose of easing injured and disabled workers back to the workplace. Rohm & Haas had 22 workers out of work for lengthy periods of time, some of which were 10 years. These workers were invited to participate in a program where they supervised mentally disabled adults doing low skilled work for Rohm & Haas in an independent company. The returned-to-work employees reduced the workers compensation burden carried by the employer. The EAP, an outside vendor, provided the advice on how Rohm & Haas should approach the disabled. The results were three fold. The mentally impaired worker was making more than the minimum wage. The employee formerly on sick leave or disability was back on the payroll. The state of Pennsylvania taxpayers also gained. They no longer had to pay for the support of these people.

The EAP is also assisting personnel facing lay off, euphemistically called downsizing. The production facility in Philadelphia laid off approximately 250 employees. A psychologist has been engaged. This person maintains an office at the plant and often attends management meetings and walks the plant floor. The EAP has also arranged for family counseling at a site near the plant.

The GTE Service Corporation is also using EAPs for the purpose of easing the problems faced by employees facing lay off. The EAPs as well as supervisory personnel are trained to look for signs of employees who are high risks for the development of reactions to the coming change in the workplace or their work standing. If the possible troubled person is identified, he or she is referred to the EAP. Management is not involved in the counseling. They are expected to identify the problem employee and contact the proper people. Occasionally, if there is an unpleasant incident or confrontation with a disgruntled employee, Critical Incident Debriefing is employed.

Digital Equipment Corporation has a program, separate from the regular EAP for the purpose of assisting former employees. Since 1991, Digital has laid off almost 20,000 employees. The EAP provided personal assistance and referral services, and counseling services for up to six months after leaving the payroll. Bruce Davidson, the overseer of the Digital EAP commented that an individual having difficulty adjusting to the new conditions needed these services before outplacement and job searching assistance could be of value (Wise, 1993, p. 40 [5]).

It should be noted here that utilizing Critical Incident Debriefing is a separate skill. It was almost always used in caring for people exposed to trauma. Firefighters are a prime example of people being exposed to this type of care. More recently Critical Incident Stress Debriefing was employed by the US Coast Guard. It was used to help those exposed to the aftermath of the crash of flight 800 in 1997. Much of the debriefing was conducted by EAPs and MAPs of the Airline. Civilian rescue workers as well as the families of the victims were offered debriefing. Recently, training in Critical Incident Stress Debriefing (CISD) was conducted in New York City. All participants, with one exception, were either EAPs or MAPs. This is another relatively new area that appears to be falling into the purview of assistance programs. In the future this assistance will certainly not be limited to those involved in emergency situations. More and more EAPs and MAPs are availing themselves to this training. Critical Incident Stress Debriefing is a method of managing stress and is described as..."a comprehensive, organized approach for the reduction and control of harmful aspects of stress in emergency services" (Mitchell & Everly, Jr., 1996, p. 28). CISD quickly became a tool for Labor Assistance Professionals within hours of September, 11, 2001. Thorough training was administered to many who had to deal with the myriad of problems stemming from the attack including what became known as "Ambiguous Loss". How do you handle the loss of a loved one when no body ahs been recovered? This became another job of Labor Assistance Professionals in their effort to 'take care of their own'.

Workplace Violence

A great deal of time has been spent investigating the cost of alcohol, drugs, stress and depression to the workplace.

Today there is another contributor to injuries and death in the work site. Workplace violence. We all know what "going postal" means. It is unfortunate that this type of behavior is, seemingly, the type of workplace violence getting publicity or notoriety. More often than not, workplace violence takes on a different appearance. It is an important issue. It is costly, and quite often extremely dangerous. Several years ago the National Organization of Women (NOW) reported that the number one cause of fatalities to women in the workplace was murder.

The work site is trying to do something about violence on the job. The reasons for the actions should be obvious. Violence looks bad. It creates a bad public image. The spin doctors have to be creative in handling this issue. Of course, there is always the corporate bottom line. Violence in the workplace affects the profit line. It is no small concern. The International Facility Management Association conducted a workplace violence survey. Of those responding, 43% admitted to violent incidents in the 3 previous years. The most common incidents are phone call of a threatening nature, bomb scares, weapons in the workplace. Fights and murder threats were all too common. These violent acts hurt by increasing absenteeism and lowering morale. Productivity is often impeded. Conflicts between labor and management arise. There are more illnesses and accidents. A worker who is threatened or feels unsafe at the job is often less productive. The bottom line is often affected through litigation resulting from the incident. Enter the EAP.

Today, many companies are taking a zero-tolerance position regarding behavior that is disruptive to the worksite. Interestingly enough, employees exhibiting such a behavioral pattern are not automatically dismissed. There are EAPs that deal with this type of situation, along with their other chores. The EAP tries to identify the problem or issue that is the catalyst for violent behavior. This includes the family as well as the employee. Services for problems such as financial woes, marital difficulties, substance abuse, and other problems are offered. Again, the EAP benefits both the employer and the employee. Businesses that do not have an EAP offering such programs have more weapon related incidents and fights. They experience more property damage. Employees in these workplace experience more threats of harm, have more attempts of harm perpetrated on them, and actually are the victims of real violence (Hess, 1996).

Two other articles (Getting Results...for the Hands-On Manager June, 1996 & HR Focus, Sept., 1996) on the subject of Workplace Violence mention ways of handling and avoiding this problem. The Occupational Safety and Health Administration (OSHA), in their guideline for handling workplace violence, recommend that managers be held responsible for preventing workplace violence. They should also be trained in the recognition and defusing of such situations. The training is necessary. No company or union should place their employees or members in harms way without seeing that they receive specialized training. They may have to defuse a situation. A zero tolerance policy should be adopted along with encouraging the reporting of incidents without fear of reprisal. A task force to examine illness and injury records is also recommended. Other suggestions are to analyze incidents, keeping an eye on trends, evaluating security. If a person is identified early on as a potential problem, he or she could be referred to the EAP or MAP.

While all this has some sound value, there are some serious difficulties facing assistance personnel dealing with this problem. For one, there is the interpretation of violence in the workplace. As a person who has some dealing with what was termed, by the company, as violence, I found serious interpretive issues. When an employee tells a manager that he or she is going to get their butt kicked or that they should have the s—- beat out of them, it is reported as a workplace violence issue. This does not occur on every occasion but it happens enough. If a burly individual with a known or even rumored history of past violence uttered those words, there should be some concern. When uttered by an employee who may be less than desirable, in the eyes of management, but has no past or rumored past of violence, we could easily see a disciplinary problem brewing. Management can and has used such incidents as a method of getting rid or disciplining such an employee. Human nature being what it is, this could be vengeful or vindictive. Personalities clash. It is not impossible to believe that the person with the power may abuse that power. A non-violent situation could escalate to a violent one. Here is where EAPs and MAPs become involved and sometimes adversarial. The employee, if not dismissed, may be sent to the EAP for evaluation. The EAP gets its information from management and for all intents is management. Even if the EAP is external, they are paid by the company. They also do not want to have a situation escalate. The MAP is also faced with a major problem. They may know of a past or rumored past history of the member. It may or may not be connected to substance abuse or mental health. The MAP still has to protect the member, just as the company has to protect the threatened or perceived to be threatened manager or fellow employee. The protection provided by the union to the member is not limited to securing the job. The protection could lie in getting the individual the necessary help required. The union has nothing to gain by seeing the workplace or other members upset or hurt by an act of violence. The difficulty lies in the interpretation of violence. I am not attempting to make light of a violent issue. If there is a true act of violence, then action needs to be taken immediately. I am focusing on mistakes and the problems caused that could grow into a truly violent incident. Care must be used by all parties in describing what is termed an incident of workplace violence. No one needs to have an off-the-cuff remark blown out of proportion. Less than proper evaluation and investigation into an alleged violation such as mentioned here could lead to a very bad incident.

A way of avoiding the problem of misinterpretation and getting proper evaluation and intervention is to make sure there are employee representatives on the workplace violence teams. Even in a non-union environment, it is important that there be a non-management representative. All the members of the team should be trained equally. The training should include recognizing circumstances that they should not become involved in. If violence is going to lead to a dismissal or suspension, the union or employee representative should not be part of the action. The reasons for this are simple. One, the union will more than likely represent the disciplined employee at a grievance hearing or future arbitration. The fellow employee is a peer. It makes sense that all parties be appraised of what ever action is to take place. A second reason why the union and fellow employee should not be part of the disciplinary proceedings is this is a violence issue. Their presence may very well escalate the proceedings to a even more violent confrontation. The employee/member being disciplined may feel that everyone is against him. The third and most obvious reason for the union or employee representative not being part of the discipline is management hires and fires in almost every instance.

The interpretation of what constitutes violent behavior and what to do about it becomes even more convoluted as time passes. A person who is mentally impaired and by virtue of that illness verbally threatens a person may be covered by the Americans With Disabilities Act (ADA). Dismissing that individual may prove extremely difficult and costly. If there is a dismissal and that person comes under the guidelines for protection under the ADA, the employer could be sued. Before disciplining an individual for workplace violence, a lot of investigation needs to be done. The act of violence may be one of self defense.

Small businesses

Misconceptions about the cost of maintaining an EAP are a big reason why some small business do not adopt assistance programs. Besides the cost they are concerned with being associated with the problems programs try to fix (Intindola, 1991). By 1996, firms with fewer than 500 employees were more likely to employ drug abusers than larger businesses. Sixty percent of the users of illicit drugs worked for these companies (Gemignani, 1997). In some instances the cost factor has been addressed after EAPs have been introduced. Discounts in workers comp insurers have been offered in to employers in 14 states that have implemented a drug-free workplace program along with EAP services. Drug testing is also included. In one survey of such companies, it was disclosed that there was a 5% cut in workers' comp premiums. Most of the recipients were in employers with less than 200 employees.

A three year study was conducted by the Washington, DC area. It looked at getting EAP services for the almost 95,000 small businesses in that area. The Corporation Against Drug Abuse (CADA) ran a project that was designed to uncover if a consortium model for the provision of EAP services was viable. A consortium, the Washington Employer Resource Consortium was formed. It provided discounted access to employee assistance and drug testing services. It also provided technical and supervisory training, information and education on the problem of substance abuse in the workplace. In the first year they had 41 small businesses as members. They wanted to improve the employer understanding of employee assistance services. They also wanted to make sure that there was a consistency in delivery service. However, in the first only 10 sought employee assistance services while 3 bought drug testing services. The consortium developed a preferred provider network for the provision of EAP assistance services. WERC recognized the need for individual training for their members. They discovered that combining groups for training was unsuccessful. They found that small employers desired individual services. By individualizing the training, the employer could select only those services that were necessary. WERC was fortunate having available in this market many small businesses with management having had prior experience with EAPs. They knew of their value in regards to improved profit and production.. CADA recognizes that the road is going to be fairly long. Only a small portion understand the how valuables EAP and related services can be. A majority of small business do not under stand their value, as of yet (Blackmon, 1996).

What we may be seeing here is the shifting sands where small businesses and assistance programs are concerned. Most large employer, those with 5,000 or more employees already have EAPs and where the unions involved and MAP. We con not forget the jointly managed assistance program. The world of small business had previously been excluded from the world of assisting their employees and their families in areas such as chemical dependency and mental health. Where they were once concerned by the costs, we have seen a methodology for reducing the cost of each small company purchasing chemical dependence and mental health coverage as part of their benefit packages. Naturally, all small businesses are not going to participate in an EAP or purchase EAP services from an outside vendor. There are, as we saw earlier, certain areas and businesses where the purchase of assistance services is not necessary. There is an ample workforce or the potential for workers is obvious. Replacing a person who, in other circumstances, would be a candidate for EAP referral can be easily managed. Of course, it would be a nice idea to have such services available but we know that there is a monetary commitment to EAPs. Unless there is a financial gain there is little or no reason to instituted EAPs.

Drug Testing

The area of drug testing raises plenty of questions and concerns for management as well as the unions. Is it necessary? Does it work? Is it cost efficient? Is it accurate? These are just some of the questions and concerns faced by the parties involved in drug testing.

The most obvious reason for drug testing has been discussed at some length. Substance abuse is costing the workplace billions upon billions of dollars a year. Insurance rates are going up. Employers would like to do away with having drug users or an alcohol abuser on their payroll. Fortunately, for the employee, once hired, they are afforded some type of protection or help. Unless the violation is a serious one, he or she will probably not be terminated for violating the drug free workplace policy. Let us not lose sight of the fact that we are speaking of illegal drugs and the word illegal speaks for itself. There is a different approach to the hiring process. Today, drug testing, especially in safety sensitive areas, is part of the pre-employment screening process. Anyone testing positive for illegal drugs will not be hired.

It is important that we all understand that drug testing is not limited to truck drivers, pilots and others is what is called safety-sensitive positions. Drug testing is gaining momentum in all walks of employment and is being supported by the courts. In an article, Supreme Court Could Usher In A Wave of Drug Testing (Alcoholism and Drug Abuse, Oct. 13, 1997), action by the courts is addressed. In early Oct., 1997 the U.S. Supreme Court refused to review the drug testing policy of Glendale CA. In Glendale, drug testing was not only mandatory for all applicants for city jobs, some employees who were candidates for promotion also had to submit to testing. Here is where the situation becomes sticky, regarding the promotion candidates. They are to be tested if the promotion they are seeking would place them in a position of public safety. The determination to test would be based on factors such as the job risk level, the possible danger to others and the applicant's personal history. Both the unions for the employees and the American Civil Liberties Union (ACLU) strongly opposed these measures. There is already a three month probation period where the employee is monitored for competence. This could allow the municipality the right to investigate what may normally be covered by confidentiality laws. Persons having received treatment for chemical dependency have a right to have their records kept confidential. This is covered in Title III, sec. 333, Public Law 91-616, enacted by the 91st Congress, dated Dec. 31, 1970. A ranking manager with prior knowledge and with a possible axe to grind may, out of revenge, recommend a person with the possibility of promotion for drug testing. Before I am perceived as being anti-management, I would like to point out that this information could come from a union source. There is a good chance that the manager with the discretionary powers to order drug testing, may have been tipped off by the union. The prospective promotion candidate may have run afoul of the union. He or she could have been an anti-union advocate or a scab. No matter how it is looked upon, the rights of the individual come into play.

This causes a dilemma for assistance professionals. EAPs, both internal and external, are paid by the employer, either singularly or through a consortium. We have to ask; where is their allegiance? Failure to comply with the wishes of those paying for the services could end up in the employers searching for a more amenable EAP. For Union MAPs, the question is the same. They owe their allegiance to the member. The problem goes deeper. Unions do not condone their membership drinking on the job or drinking, to such a degree, that the drinking endangers the public, other union members or management. Their stance is the same on the use of illegal drugs. All assistance professionals are concerned. When it comes to unions, many people are under the misapprehension that unions will fight drug testing. They will, if it is wrong and in violation of a workers rights. However, if it is necessary and lawful unions will comply. Hartwell, Steele, and Rodman (1996) tell us that almost 13% of businesses having a work force of 50 or more are represented by unions. A workplace with a larger percentage of unionized employees is more likely to have drug testing than other businesses.

There are several gray areas in the world of drug testing. One which should cause great concern is that drug testing does not establish impairment. It shows a person has used illegal drugs or within a certain amount of past time but does not say what effect was experienced by the user. This presents an extra added problem since alcohol testing can detect impairment. The problem here is in who is drunk or impaired and who is not. Spend some time in court and listen to the questions asked of a Police Officer who has affected the arrest of a person for impaired driving or driving while intoxicated. The amount of alcohol present in an individual can be scientifically measured. Despite being a good indicator as to who is and who is not drunk, it is not always correct as to every individual. The testimony of the Police Officer is often critical, despite how high the level of alcohol is. A person may test at or above the recognized limit determining being intoxicated. That does not concretely prove the individual is in fact drunk while driving. The Police Officer may have to testify that he gave a physical sobriety test. The person may have walked the line perfectly, spoken without slurring, found his nose with his index finger with eyes closed, and responded rationally to all the questions posed by the Officer. That person may not be drunk or impaired. I do not suggest that just because a person has a greater tolerance for alcohol than another that it ok for him or her to drive. I use this as an example to show that testing is not always correct.

Pre-employment screening also poses a problem. It can not indicate long term alcohol abuse. It can not, therefore, indicate how a person will perform on the job. If a person believes that he or she is to be going for a job interview in the near future and testing is likely, they choose to abstain from alcohol for a few days. The test will show negative results. All drugs will not dissipate in a few short hours or days. Marijuana will show up from 15 to 30 days or longer. The length of time it remains in ones' system is in proportion to how much and how long it is used. Again, the test will only show usage, not effect. Other drugs, like cocaine and heroin will leave the body much more quickly that marijuana.

Omnibus Transportation Employee Testing Act.

This act passed in 1991 required the testing of employees in safety sensitive positions Air line pilots, operators of mass transit travel trains and busses, railroad engineers and other motor carriers were required to be tested. Since November 1998, there had been rules on the books regarding drug and alcohol testing. These rules were to be implemented by large employers, those having 50 or more employees by January 1, 1995. All others had until January 1, 1996 to implement drug and alcohol testing policies. The numbers are large. The Federal Highway Administration estimated that the new regulations will affect approximately 300,000 companies. Of all industries, they largest covered by the act are employees of motor carriers. A company whose driver operate vehicles weighing 26,001 pounds or having a weight rating 26,001 pounds or more, including a towed unit with a weight rating of 10,000 pounds or more; operate vehicles transporting 16 or more passengers including the driver; operating vehicles carrying hazardous waste, must create substance abuse policies. These policies include random testing for alcohol and five classes of drugs. They must also provide supervisory training and written information be provided to safety sensitive employees. They must also adhere to the requirements for specific record keeping and reporting. To help insure that the testing is taking place, there are penalties for failed compliance. Owners of companies that fail to adhere to the rules can have their operating licenses pulled. They also face the possibility of criminal penalties. They can also be fined up to $10,000 a day for rule violation (Fenn, Feb., 1996; Sinclair, March 1996; Morton, Jan. 1997).

Who gets tested?

The job of train engineer, bus or truck driver is usually referred to a blue collar work. Is the blue collar worker picked on are they treated equally compared to the white collar worker? According to Boles, (1997), there is a great disparity in testing workers. SAMHSA conducted a survey of full time workers from the ages of 18 to 49. What they found show a fairly large degree of disparity. The number of blue collar workers tested is much higher than their white collar counterparts. Full time workers aged 18 to 49 were asked if they had been subjected to mandatory drug testing is the previous year. The responses indicated that the trucking services industry had the highest percentage of tests, 45.5%. Those involved in air transport were tested at the rate of 40.8%, while sanitation workers and utility workers were tested at the rate of almost 40%. Even those involved in the grocery business were tested at the rate of 28.7%. The other side of the coin is entirely different regarding mandatory testing. Those involved in the field of legal services were tested at the rate of 2.2%. In the field of education the rating 2.5% of a group that consists of employees in colleges, business schools and universities and 3.8% for those involved in elementary and secondary schools. There may be a perceived idea or prejudice that only blue collar workers are drug addicts or alcoholics. SAMHSA has several publications that will show you that the relationship to educated and uneducated, college graduates or college attendee, and those having no college are somewhat similar. There has been a change in the demographics in recent years. The bottom line is that there are more than enough drug and alcohol users and abusers in the workplace than we believe there are. Many Wall Street firms, banks, insurance companies, and other traditionally white collar employers have EAPs. R. H. Macy, in 1917, sponsored the first ever employee counseling program. This was followed in 1919 by Metropolitan Life Insurance Company (Sonnenstuhl & Trice, 1986, p. 10).

Does drug testing work?

The answer is not just a simple yes or no. Life would easier if there were no conflicts. Drug testing is no different. It causes conflicting opinions. If the concern was to identify drug users and abusers, then the testing works. We are looking at the problems of alcohol and drugs and how it impacts workers, the workplace, and the unions. Most companies are not in business because they have a social conscience. They are in business to make money. They do not want to waste money. They have to weigh the costs of testing.

In an article in the National Underwriter (Apr. 4, 1994) it is reported that a survey conducted by the William Mercer Company indicated that many employers are testing job candidates and employees. The results show they are not finding many abusers. The report also states that among job applicants tested, the positive results have dropped over the previous 3 years. Maltby, (Mar. 1998) gives us another view in regards to cost vs. effectiveness. Four years after the report on William Mercers' survey, the new information confirms the findings in staggering numbers. Texas Instrument tested 1,000 employees at a cost of $1 million. They found 49 employees testing positive. The cost for uncovering these 49 employees was $20,000 each. The AMA reports a cost of $10,000 for their testing of the membership. This brings us back to who and who does not get tested. It may be worth the expense to uncover problem employees in safety sensitive positions. People may have to ask themselves is; is it worth the money spent on drug testing to see which white collar worker did a little coke or smoked some marijuana over the weekend? No need to speak ideologically on this issue. There are sure to be several opinions.

There are other, less expensive ways of identifying who is and who is not a substance abuser. For years, observation has been a good method of checks and balances. EAPs and MAPs have been successful. Recall there is a major difference between the two programs. The union can act on rumor. This is valuable. Many working in the white collar arena may have observed co-worker leaving the men's' or ladies' room with a white powdery substance under the nose. I am not the only person who has seen or heard of a person emerging from the toilet with a stain of blood coming through the elbow portion of the shirt or blouse, or having blood trickle down an arm. We usually know who goes the bar near the workplace and drinks his or her lunch. Another way of avoiding the costs of drug testing is to make it common knowledge that testing will be done after accidents and that those testing positive will face extreme difficulties and possible dismissal. Letting prospective employees know that they will have to be tested can also help alleviate the problem of hiring abusers.

Employers may be chasing their tails in regards to drug testing. The National Institute on Drug Abuse (NIDA) has reported that the use of illegal drugs peaked in 1979. At that time 14% of all Americans over 12 reported using some sort of illegal drug in the previous month. By 1996 the figure dropped to 6%. NIDA also provides figures supporting the findings from Texan Instrument and the AMA, regarding cost and uncovering abusers. The report from NIDA says that of all random drug tests, only 3% indicate a positive result. Mark Rothstein of the Health Law and Policy Institute at the University of Houston estimates that approximately 99% of persons testing positive are casual marijuana users. The National Academy of Sciences reported, after reviewing available evidence, that an employee whose uses drugs off the job is no more likely to have an accident on-the-job than the other employees. Naturally, the more often a drug is used, the more likely it is to test positive. Lewis (April. 1996) in a report in the Brown University Digest of Addiction Theory & Application says that daily drug use consists of using drugs 228 days a year. That person has a 90% chance of testing positive on a Monday, if we assume that most drug use will take place on the weekend. The percentage drops to a low of 69% if tested on a Thursday. If a person falls into the category of a monthly user, 43 days a year, the percentages change to 27% on Monday and 7.8% on Thursday. The report indicates another classification of drug usage, annual. A person using drugs 7 days a year has percentages of being tested positive rated at 4% on Monday and less than 1% for any other week day. These figures gain more importance when we discover that the annual drug user makes up 55% of the population that uses illegal drugs. This 55% will test positive 7% of the time. 52% of daily drug users will check positive but they only make up 8% of workers. The report then says that the estimated drug use may be 8 times the rate identified by random testing. They feel that if testing is designed to intervene with the heavy drug user and to discourage the casual user, they can expect to find that testing can do both. I feel that we can not overlook the fact that, up until now, only alcohol testing will test for impairment. Donna Bush, Ph. D. is the chief of drug testing for the Center for Substance Abuse Prevention's workplace programs division. She reports that "it is virtually impossible to test people for impairment by such substances as marijuana, heroin and cocaine" (Curley, April 21, 1997). The instruments used for drug screening can only tell whether an individual, sometime in the past, has used illegal drugs. This appears to be even more complicated when we look at the federal regulations on workplace testing. While alcohol can be measured, the government said that the use of illegal drugs constitutes abuse. The concept of a drug free workplace is one of preventing drug use in the workplace. They are not interested in impairment. This brings up another area of concern. With the advent of hair testing, a method of screening for drugs, the window for testing positive can be up to 90 days or more (Curley, April 21, 1997). This causes a problem. A person involved in an on-the-job accident or incident could test positive for a certain drug taken months in the past. That usage may have nothing to do with this particular event yet the employee could face disciplinary sanctions up to and including dismissal. This brings up the issue of dismissal without cause and a problem for unions representing the employee. The stance by the government on use is abuse is problematic at the very least. The question could be raised as to whether the employer, with the blessing of the federal regulations, is becoming the conscience of the country. There is also the possibility of false-positives and differences in test analyzing. That will soon be looked at.

Illegal drug use is not the only issue in decline. In colonial times, 6 gallons of alcohol were consumed by the average person annually. The alcohol consumption rose to 9.5 gallons per capita by 1830. Today it is estimated that only 2.8 gallons of alcohol is consumed by the average person on an annual basis. Comparing 1830 to 1978 we see that 2.6 gallons of alcohol was consumed per person, annually compared to the 9.5 gallons (Lender & Martin, 1987, p. 14).

Earlier, I spoke of EAPs and MAPs and small business. It is important that they also get involved in some kind of drug testing. We know that 70% of all drug users are employed. What is really interesting is that 80% of the entire workhorse is employed in small companies (Daniels, June 23, 1997) Ms. Daniels reports on a study of conducted on 170 large policy holders serviced by the Louisiana Workers' Compensation Corp. The study indicated that there was a significant reduction in accident rates and compensation losses costs. A comparison of companies with and without drug testing showed that companies without drug testing policies had almost 60% more accidents. To offset the ill will brought about by drug testing the Compensation recommended that companies implement EAPs. This would help users to get help before they were found out and were subject to disciplinary action. They also recommended that all the firms get the approval of their legal advisors.

The recommending of review by the lawyers is sound advice given the possible problem regarding privacy. The courts show a greater sympathy and greater willingness to support pre-employment testing. The courts see random testing as more intrusive of the person who is already employed. The employee is seen as having more privacy rights than a person seeking employment. The courts try to balance the right of the employer's need for information against the expectation of privacy of the employee. Employees should be notified of a random drug testing policy. If they clearly understand that they are subject to testing they have less of a reason to expect privacy (Flynn, Apr. 1996).

Despite the debate about who gets tested and who does not, and the legal issues, drug testing does seem to be doing its job. Jack Dempsey is the head of EAP Services for the most of the construction workers in the Philadelphia, PA area. They number approximately 60,000. In addressing the monthly NYC EAPA chapter meeting Sept. 22, 1998, he stated that drug testing is saving millions of dollars annually in workers' compensation. This is not an isolated incident.

> The good news: positive drug test results have decreased among both U.S. workers and job seekers in general, according to the ninth annual AMA survey on workplace drug testing and drug abuse policies. One possible explanation for this drop is an increase in random testing. But even companies that test only on suspicion of use have reported fewer positive results. The survey included 1,151 American firms, employing more than 5 million workers (Axelrod, 1995, p. 7).

The assistant director of the American Trucking Association's safety department, Joel Dandrea feels drug testing will continue to be an important part of motor carriers safety programs if it is managed properly. Dandrea says incidents of alcohol and drug use has always been low among truck drivers. Since the numbers of drivers coming up with positive results are low, there is the possibility that the random testing of 50% be reduced. "...Federal Register which indicates that the Research and Special Programs Administration has just reduced their random rate for drug testing from 50% to 25% on an annual basis for calendar year 1997" (Morton, Jan. 1997, pp. 68-70). This should reduce the cost of drug testing. Lower cost for drug testing was also addressed by Mary Bernstein, director of the Office of Drug and Alcohol Policy and Compliance at the U.S. Department of Transportation (DOT). While she agrees that testing costs have gone down. Ms. Bernstein feels this has to do with the process maturing since the inception. She also said there were no major drug related incidents since the introduction of the DOT regulations with the noted exceptions of the Chevy Chase MD train accident and the accident in the NYC subway (Macdonald & Springer, July/Aug. 1998).

It appears that drug testing is not only hear, it is effective. Despite some obvious objections, it has gained in approval. Companies want it as part of their overall drug free workplace policy and EAP. Unions are dealing with it. Their concern is for their member's rights as well as the public's safety. Besides the obvious problems around the privacy and safety issues, there are issues surrounding the types of testing and the legality of testing.

Another indicator that drug testing in the workplace is working is in looking at acceptance. Testing is still an emotional issue but the emotions have changed. The worker of today, compared to 6 years ago is adjusting to testing and often approves of it. In 1992 they felt it was an invasion of privacy and should only be done for cause or suspicion or as part of an accident investigation. Fewer of today's employees see drug testing as an issue of invasion of privacy. Many of them feel the companies should broaden the scope of testing in an effort to improve workplace safety and productivity. One reason for the acceptance is more and more employees and managers have come to accept that testing is much more accurate today. They do not fear that they will be branded as drug users and abusers. Another reason is the economy. The relatively tight job market makes the non-user even more resentful of the user. Concern over safety is another issue. Managers and employees are concerned about safety problems that could be caused by substance abusers. They are more concerned about this than the privacy issue.

In a unionized surrounding, these issues make it easier for the union to come to an agreement with the employer. There is also present the fact after years of interaction between employers, employees, and substance abusers, the climate has changed. People in the workplace are looking at drug abusers as criminals and these criminals should not be protected by absence of drug testing. The fact that 45% of the readers of Industry Week believe there should be random drug testing. Seventy percent of employees feel all employees should be subjected to drug testing. Both these percentages are much higher than the previous survey indicated. Some attitudes have not changed. There are a great number of managers as well as employees who feel that a company using drug testing should provide rehabilitation through EAPs. The employee feeling around testing is that it should extend to management, also (Verespej, 1992).

Testing hair for chemicals

Using hair fibers for the purposes of testing is not new. The FBI has been doing it for some time and is reported to be more reliable that the urine test. One of the advantages for the employer is that hair-follicle testing can indicate when the drug had been taken. It can also give a better picture regarding the history of use. Unlike urinalysis, hair testing can detect drug use over a longer period of time. Opiates, methamphetamine, and cocaine are metabolized fairly rapidly. If a person has prior knowledge of a pending drug test and remains free of these drugs for 3 to 4 days, there is little chance that drugs will be detected. Hair testing is more exact. After a drug is taken, it travels through the blood stream. It finds its' way to the hair follicle cell. The rug becomes permanently locked in the hair. Each subsequent use of a rug becomes chronologically registered.

Since hair grows approximately one half inch a month it is easy to discover when the drug was taken. The fair follicle test will also disclose the increase of drug use. Conversely, it should indicate a decrease, if any. Unlike abstaining from drug use for a few days in urine testing, there is really no way of getting away from hair testing. Shaving ones' head will not help. Any hair from any part of the body will do. There are problems with hair testing. True, it is easier to handle than urine, there is little or no embarrassment but there are downsides. For one, every body does not grow hair at one half inch a month. Some grow longer and some shorter. There are cutoff standards in urine testing but no standards in hair testing. It is a lot more expensive than urine analysis, three times more expensive. The cost will probably go down with increased use of hair testing. Despite the perception that hair tests less intrusive than urine testing, 97% of drug testing still is done by urinalysis. There is a problem with collection. The preferred method of getting hair it to pluck it not cut it. Cutting the hair close will not disclose recent drug use. Here is a contradiction in testing. You can avoid detection by avoiding certain drugs for 3 or 4 days when it comes to urine testing. If a hair test is the order of the day and it is not plucked but cut, it will not detect current use. It takes 5 to 7 days for hair to grow. There is still a debate of genetic materials showing up as false-positives. African Americans are complaining that their hair grows more slowly therefore the testing is biased. As these debates continue, improvements in testing continue on (Alcoholism and Drug Abuse Week, 7/29/96; Brady, Feb. 1997).

Drug testing: Is it legal?

Since drug testing is a federal regulation, it stands to reason that it is legal. There are some question about legality and application. In the 1980s there were lawsuits challenging the right of the employer to test. For the most part, those issues have been resolved. Private employers can perform pre-employment testing along with testing those involved in accidents and random drug testing. The cases litigated today are concerned how the test is done and not on whether the employer can test.

Still, employers need to be careful. They need to be aware of the potential problems of defamation, privacy rights violations along with violating the Americans With Disabilities Act (ADA) or the Civil Rights Act. Regarding pre-employment screening and the ADA:

> For pre-employment screening, the ADA requires that medical exams not be done before the applicant has received a conditional offer of employment, but it specifically excludes drug tests. However, many companies hoping to avoid defamation suits retain a medical review officer to examine test results and possibly talk with the person concerned, to see if there's an innocent explanation for a positive test result. In some interpretation, that turns a drug test into a medical exam. "Prudence dictates extending a conditional offer," Segal Says. "So does common sense. There is no reason to incur the cost and concomitant risk of a test if the applicant is not otherwise qualified" (Bahls. Mar. 1998).

Bahls (1998) also tell us that Segal a lawyer in Philadelphia, PA recommends employers test right after the conditional offer is made. This would make it harder for the prospective employee to cleanse his or her system of illegal drugs. Segal also says it is a lot harder to remove an employee that it is to keep an applicant out. In dealing in a union environment the testing is subject to collective bargaining. Management can not just establish random testing without first notifying the union and bargaining testing. Segal feels that the unions "bitterly oppose random testing" and will only grudgingly accept testing n the grounds of reasonable suspicion. This appears to be a blanket statement and we have already seen that the construction workers in Philadelphia PA have endorsed testing. Other unions have addressed. The Communications Workers of America, in the North East, agreed to testing outside of the normal bargaining period. They did not wait for it to become an issue at the bargaining table. It stretches the imagination to believe that the Teamsters would allow testing, as indicated in the ATA without some kind of approval. Congress made sure that a substance abuser can not hide behind the ADA. If an employee is discharged for inappropriate conduct, that employee can not blame the action on substance abuse. If a person with a history of substance abuse poses a direct threat to others, that person can be fired. Drug testing may be administered to person in recovery to make sure that they are no longer using. On that point, some unions are going to take an issue. Is there cause or is this harassment?

Just because drug testing is legal and persons found using illegal drugs are breaking the law, arbitrators often side with the employee who has been disciplined, especially if the discipline is termination. They are not overly sympathetic toward an employer who dismisses the employee over a drug related issue. They, the arbitrators have been known to seek ways of avoiding the most serious of disciplines. They say the discipline is too much for such an offense or look for an error in the procedure.

The fact that drug testing can not measure impairment comes into play in the courts. There are offenses which can lead to dismissal even if it is a first time offense. Stealing from the employer is one example. Intoxication in the workplace can also lead to a first time offense dismissal. Intoxication seems to be the key word. Drug testing does not indicate impairment, intoxication, or any other state. It just says the person has, in the past, taken an illegal drug. There may be absolutely no indication of drug use. Employers do not necessarily want to be known as going on witch hunts. They are not, as I stated before, the social conscience of the country. Leniency could go a long way in the event that their testing policy subjected to court scrutiny. Many employers recognize this and have instituted rehabilitation programs through their EAP (Flynn, Apr. 1996). There is also the possibility of getting the person to admit he or she needs help. Let us not forget the coercion that can be put forth by the union or the management. The employer can say they can not tolerate this behavior and give the person the opportunity to clean up the act. They can let the employee know that there is no third chance. The union can then say, they have done all they could. They will agree to fight the dismissal. They can also tell the member that it has been their experience that the company usually wins in this type of case. It comes down to which is stronger, the desire to retain employment and support the family or succumb to the force of denial.

Testing and the unions

The employer can test all applicants. He can not test all employees. Even where the federal regulations are in place, the employer must negotiate with the unions in order to test for drugs. Even if the employer has rules in place such as fitness for duty or has broad managing rights clause. The employer does not have a duty to bargain the testing for alcohol or other drugs. They do have the duty to bargain when it comes to testing those already of the payroll. Many employers do not realize that this duty exists. If a company decides that it only wants to test once, it must be bargained for. Testing poses a problem for some unions. Despite the fact they recognize the need for some type of testing they may have a tough time convincing the entire rank and file that this is a good idea. If the anti testing feeling was strong enough, the company may have to remove it from bargaining. There are not many companies that are willing to risk a strike over drug testing. In order to sell the idea of testing, the employer may have to give up more money than he wants to. He may have to sweeten the deal. To avoid both problems, many times bargaining for testing is not done at the usual bargaining rounds but at a different time. There are times when drug testing can be discussed at the regularly scheduled bargaining period. If it is already part of the collective bargaining agreement or if there is a statement of complete understanding between the parties. A company could have an agreement that it can test for cause or reasonable suspicion. They can not get into random testing without negotiating with the union. If the contract is silent, meaning there is no language in the present contract, "the issue usually can be raised midterm, and upon impasse, implemented unilaterally". Unions involved in negotiations around testing will almost always argue for giving the employee another test after having a positive result. If there is no provision for EAP in place, they may ask for one. They will certainly want their member to use the services of the union MAP. At this point, I do not feel it is necessary to go back and review how much is saved through the implementation of EAP and MAP services. We also have seen how the courts feel about overly severe discipline. It, to, becomes costly. And it is the right thing to do, in the light of trying to maintain a decent working relationship with the union.

In workplaces having both union and non-union employees, those not represented by the union are subjected to testing before the unionized employees. This is done because it is easier and in the hopes that the union will not resist too strenuously after the non union people have been tested. This could backfire on the employer. There is always the possibility of the testing being modified as a result of bargaining with the union. The non-union employees may decide to become unionized, seeking the protection offered by the union and the collective bargaining agreement.

The union management relationship on drug testing becomes even more complicated. Employers are required by law to furnish a safe workplace. Providing this may entail drug testing for suspicion or with cause. This, as far as unions are concerned, protects the rights of the majority of the membership. A problem with reasonable suspicion or for cause testing is just what constitutes reasonable suspicion or for cause. Management can easily abuse their powers since just about any negative observation can fall into those categories. With this in mind, some union leaders are in favor of random testing believing that random testing will lead to less frequent random testing. The down side of random drug testing is that it often leads people to feel insecure. There is the feeling of anxiety and of being oppressed.

In dealing with union in regards to testing as a result of reasonable suspicion or for cause, there are certain recommendations. One is that the test is based on suspicion from a person not normally the regular supervisor. The second is to notify the shop or floor steward who should be able to observe the reason for the suspicion. The third is to inform supervisory personnel that they will admonished if they abuse their power regarding recommending testing for reasonable suspicion or for cause (Segal, Dec. 1991).

All three recommendations pose problems. First, there is a real possibility of misjudgment on the part of supervisor unfamiliar with the person observed. If this outside manager is brought in on the observation and request of the subjects' immediate supervisor, then why not just use the shop or floor steward as recommended. The second issue is the use of the shop or floor steward. What happens if there is a difference of opinion or if the steward knows of some information that may have the employee acting in a rather strange manner that has nothing to do with chemical use or dependency? The information that may be known by the steward may be of a confidential nature. This puts the steward in an awkward position. He or she must either divulge the reason or allow their member to be subjected to a drug test. If that particular steward is a union peer counselor, the predicament is even worse. There is no way the steward should reveal that information, even if the behavior is not chemically induced. The third piece could be the most important. Drug testing although important, is still a point of strong contention by many unions. They are not necessarily against drug testing for cause. They just do not want to see the rights of privacy taken away by whimsy or personal dislikes or prejudices. The penalty for management abuse should be as public as the testing policy. Everyone should know about the policy and all should have equal knowledge of the penalties for abusing the power of test recommendations.

Summary

EAPs and MAPs have been successful and they will be needed in the future. Their tasks will remain the same and they will change. They will always have the one common thread. They both work for people and they service people. We have seen some of the changes already taking place and what and how EAPs and MAPs are helping. Fifteen years ago I doubt there were any assistance professionals worrying about how they were going to handle the problems of an employee or union member and their families in the world of downsizing or layoffs. Construction workers work hard but often sporadic. They are used to layoffs. They become inured to that part of their life. They do not like it but they know it is not only a possibility, it is a probability. Not so the factory worker or white collar worker. They felt they would have cradle to the grave employment and benefits. Layoffs to them were as foreign as the dark side of the moon. Layoffs only happen in insecure businesses or in construction, not in banks and the automotive industries. EAPs and MAPs not only helped these people in their hour of need they even helped get some people back on the payrolls. This is a far cry from what the traditional views of assistance programs were in the past.

Workplace violence has also come to the attention of EAPs and MAPs. We have seen the problems with misunderstandings being taken out of proportion and escalated to extremes. We have also seen how MAPs and EAPs are involved. There is a need for properly trained individuals to deal with these issues. Many times this will fall under the umbrella of the assistance professionals. After all, they are used to dealing with the employees and the membership in adverse or uncomfortable conditions. The difference of the loyalties of EAPs and MAPs were mentioned and was not intended to disparage any assistance professional. I mention this as a warning of the possibilities of danger in supporting what may be unfounded or misinterpreted reports of violence. By the same token, incidents and reports of possible workplace violence must be investigated thoroughly. There are real dangers to life and health in our daily lives and the workplace is part of our daily lives. We need to be as safe at work just as we try to be safe at home.   S m a l l businesses are also becoming more aware of the benefits of having EAPs. There are many smaller companies now using the services of external EAPs. Small companies have formed coalitions or consortiums for the purpose of getting program help for their employees. EAPs and in some instances MAPs are no longer the province of large companies. Most people are employed by what are categorized as small companies. We often think differently about employment. We often overlook the fact regarding employment and the small company.

Of all the problems facing the EAPs and the MAPs is the future as well as today none is more perplexing than the issue of drug testing. Management wants it. Often the unions want it. Both entities realize that drug testing leads to a safer workplace. The statistics mentioned show how drug testing has been impacting the. Less accidents translates into less compensation, leading to a lessening of compensation premiums. Less absences due to accidents, means more productivity. The problems lie in who gets tested and how the testing is done. Management wants to test everyone and the unions have reservations. Privately and often openly, all unions are not against drug testing. We have seen some unions accepting and even favoring drug testing. They are concerned with the right to privacy, abuse of testing, and having testing done as a method of harassing an employee. MAPs and EAPs are having difficulties in dealing with hair testing which shows use but not abuse, prior use but not impairment. All are having difficulty with hair testing being challenged as being prejudiced toward minorities because their hair grows slower than whites. The decline in what used to be called cradle-to-the-grave employment often leads to workers who know they are drug free to call for the testing of fellow workers. They want to use drug testing as a method for retention of their jobs at the expense of others. The public believes that everyone should be tested. They think everyone is in a safety sensitive job. These are the same people who rail at the prospects of having their children tested. I do not want to go off in a different direction here. It is safe to say that the adage of being careful in what you ask for. Many who feel that business and government already have too much of a say in the everyday life experience are sitting around watching another intrusion. They are being victimized by the paranoia of facing drug addicts and alcoholics flying planes. This is true. There are drug addicts everywhere. Occasionally, there are incidents of intoxicated pilots. But does this fact give employers to test each and every employee on a whim? This is the concern of the unions and their MAPs. There are other methods of determining who is and who is not a drug abuser or alcoholic that do not require drug testing. Pre-employment screening and scrutiny during probationary periods of employment should give a better view of who is and who is not a problem. There are fewer users of illegal drugs today than in the past. No testing can indicated what will happen down the line. The future is not made clear by testing. We have also seen where testing is no longer the useful tool it once was. Maybe the message has been received. Most people do not want to lose a job as a result of failing a drug screening test. There may be a common ground where EAPs, MAPs, and the employer can meet and put this issue in the proper light. Until that time, EAPs and MAPs will struggle along and deal with this change in times just as they have done for almost 200 years.

CHAPTER 10

We have seen great changes in the field of treatment. Drug testing is here, workplace violence is on the rise, drugs, like heroin, cocaine, and alcohol have been joined by new, designer drugs. New regulations and treatment options have been introduced. Labor realized that the Assistance Program Personnel had to learn about legal issues to protect both the member and or his/her family and to protect themselves and their unions. When these changes became evident, professionalism increased. The traditional Union or Member Assistance Personnel had to change, keeping up with the times, and the people. Labor Assistance Professionals recognized these changes and realized they too had to become more educated, far beyond their traditional knowledge. Peer Assistance is still the core of LAP but it had to be augmented by increased knowledge and professionalism. They knew they could not avoid Drug Testing. They knew that they had to gather more knowledge in an effort to not only protect their members but to protect their rights. They had to learn about the pharmacology of drugs. There are actually more female union members than male members, leading labor to become more proactive and educated regarding women and their problems.

After many years of very hard work and research people like Ted Mapes, Heather Healy, Don Perks, Jack Freckman, Tom Cole, Bob Belaire, and others in conjunction with the National Labor College unveiled an educational program for Union Assistance People by Union Assistance Program People. Their training is clear, concise and most importantly, extremely professional in course material leading to Middle States Accreditation for college credits along with a Nationally Recognized Certification, LAP-C. The training is conducted by college teachers, attorneys, Ph.Ds, Union Assistance Directors, all schooled in the area of Labor Assistance Professionalism. Labor Assistance Professionals rose to the occasion.

Labor Assistance Professionals

LAP has become more than a group peer counselors. MAPs in the past weren't particularly interested in bargaining or influencing bargaining. The truly successful MAPs stayed out of the union political scene. Today with the erosion of benefits, the MAPs are learning how to present to their executive boards on getting new or keeping present coverage. This often involves to all parties that they aren't getting the benefits they bargained. Other new areas are covered by LAP in the process of making LAP members and Union Assistance Plans more effective and knowledgeable. Listing and talking a bout the entire LAP curriculum would be extremely long so we'll look at just a few achievements in the expanding LAP driven professionalism

Drug Testing

Many people watch televisions shows about police officers and how they do their jobs. We have three current shows on crime scene investigations and evidence processing. What has that to do with Labor Assistance Professionals? A great deal. If we listen to the shows we know the absolute importance of maintaining the 'chain of evidence'. Evidence must never leave the sight or control to the persons responsible for such material. This task has also fallen into the work of Labor Assistance Professionals, along with assuring that the 'evidence' hasn't been tampered with or the worker impugned by false positives.

To many Labor Professionals the 'chain of evidence', or custody chain is something new. Collection procedures must be maintained. There is the responsibility to protect the member from being tainted by mishandled test samples which is just as important in protecting them from false positives. We also note that some substances can be misinterpreted. This causes another problem for workers and Assistance Professionals. To coin a rather famous New York phrase; Who Knew? Some LAP members knew and were making sure that the rest of labor had the opportunity to learn to foster the tradition of 'labor taking care of its own'.

We all know the meaning of 'false positives' but what would you do if the result of your drug test was accurate, but the conclusion surround the meaning of the result was inaccurate? As validity testing surfaced in the late 1990s, many unions, especially the largest union representing Flight Attendants (The Association of flight Attendants) started experiencing the termination of their members for "cheating" on their drug tests. According to a new lab procedure called "substitution testing", labs were pairing the creatinine and specific gravity levels of all urine samples to determine if the donations were "human urine." If a sample's creatinine and specific gravity fell below the cutoff levels recommended by the Drug Testing Advisory Board and then adopted by the Federal government, than the donor was deemed to have substituted her or his urine. According to the "experts" that established the cutoff levels for Federal Drug Testing, no human could produce a urine sample with a creatinine level below their established bar without being fatally ill or being a cheater. Substituting one's urine is considered a refusal to test and typically carries the penalty of termination under most employer policies. To AFA's dismay, they were having members with no prior substance abuse history and no reason for cheating on a urine drug test being terminated for urine results measuring below the established creatinine level. They were being fired as "cheaters" on their drug tests. After extensive research, it was clear that low creatinine levels were in part a function of small body size, low muscle mass, routine water consumption, and possibly diets high in plant matter. This information lead AFA to begin concluding that their primarily female membership that always drinks water to compensate for their dehydrating work environment, was an occupational group at risk of termination because of faulty science underpinning the established cut off levels for creatinine. AFA began to work with terminated flight attendants to simulate their normal water drinking habits and then administered DOT look a like drug tests to them. AFA produced evidence that healthy flight attendants could in fact reproduce under direct medical observation low level creatinine samples well below the cut off levels that the Federal government said was "humanly impossible". As a result, the regulated creatinine thresholds for substitution testing was formally lowered by 250% to minimize the continued adverse job consequences for non-cheating employees. Many of the AFA flight attendants have been returned to their positions. But today, employees who were terminated before the creatinine levels were lowered have yet to be provided formal notice of the government's error or a remedy for the injustice done to them. The federal government committed to offering these victims a process but nothing has yet come forward after all these years. Who knew about creatinine and false positives and the problems of 'chain of evidence? Heather Healy, with the Association of Flight Attendants Member Assistance Program who spear-headed AFA;'s efforts.

This incident is just one of many areas in which MAPs have become more professional. What would have happened just 5 short years ago when a certified lab returned accurate information based on the sample tested that the sample was altered? Case closed. Who would take on a certified lab where the custody chain was intact? A strong Union Assistance Program. In the first case the accused insisted she was innocent. This was a motivator. We all know that managers at the grievance table and arbitrators at hearings hold with the belief that the company has no reason to lie while the employee has reason. The company didn't lie and neither did the dismissed member. Heather took protecting her members to new levels. She took on the system. This information was and continues to be shared with all LAP members at conferences and through the LAP educational courses at the National Labor College. Newer and older MAPs are improving, and are better informed and educated through LAP.

The LAP Course is exposing the members to things they rarely considered in the past. There was drug testing and unions had to go along with that decision, for the most part. Now labor people are taught the importance of making sure the testing is done by a lab and personnel are by certified the National Institute of Drug Abuse (NIDA). They know that the labs can be wrong, even when they follow procedures, as we have seen. They also have to deal with Medical Review Officers, their qualifications and their scope of authority. LAP members are advised to become certified as Substance Abuse Professionals (SAPs). A SAP can overrule the decisions of the MRO regarding testing and going back to work. It is not my intention to list all the components involved in the evolving area of union involvement in drug testing and protecting the members. The intent is to indicate the knowledge needed in the MAP work world and who is taking charge to see the information is disseminated.

Pharmacology

MAP/UAPs were well versed in alcohol and drugs use, abuse and addiction. We knew alcohol was the most common and most dangerous of all drugs. We knew about heroin, cocaine, heroin and other drugs. In today's world, that is not enough. Ten years ago, steroids were strictly the drug for athletes. Not any longer.

Date Rape and Predatory Drugs are fairly new to the traditional Assistance Professionals. LAP is on top of educating its members on these new drugs, drugs that are more openly taken.

A study of the growing number of minorities in the workplace is a topic entirely too broad to be included in this work. It is sufficient to say that Labor people are well aware of the influx of these people and the cultural differences they bring with them. Their history shows that they, so far, have been less likely to have received any treatment for chemical dependency, yet their workplace numbers grow. Some bring in new drugs and cultural acceptance to that drug. Khat is one such drug.

It is native to East Africa and the Arabian Peninsula. Use of Khat can lead to suicide, violence and exhaustion. It certainly reduces productivity. A problem facing LAP in the future, with the increase of people from Africa and the Middle East will be that Khat is legal in many parts of the world.

LAP incorporates information from the Drug Enforcement Administration in an effort to keep abreast of newer more dangerous drugs, either entering or manufactured right here.

We know that drugs such as PCP, Methamphetamine, Gamma Hydroxybutyric Acid (GHB), also known as GHB,(Grievous Bodily Harm), more commonly known as Ecstasy, are produced in small mobile labs, or in homes, and readily available for distribution. Ecstasy and other predatory drugs are so available that when over 14 million tabs are recovered by authorities, not a single beat is missed in the distribution and use chain.

Drugs change, distribution and manufacturing becomes easier, the age of the user and the frequency and place of usage may change. The one thing that is constant is LAP is keeping up with the changes, making certain that the people charged with the task of 'taking care of our own' are up to the task with the latest information. We know we can't get ahead of drugs and alcohol but we can keep up with the change, through the passing of knowledge.

Law

Regarding legal issues, MAPs know their responsibilities regarding confidentiality from the professional and legal point of view. The confidentiality became law in the 1970 with the Comprehensive Alcohol Abuse and Alcoholism Prevention, Treatment, and Rehabilitation Act and again in 1974 with Title 1-Federal Assistance for State and Local Alcoholism and Alcohol Abuse Programs, but like most things in life there are changes that require more understanding and action. Confidentiality can and must be broken, by law, in certain. Duty to Warn in cases involving elder abuse, child abuse, a danger to self or another or court order can mandate violating confidentiality. Not only that but we are now obligated to warn a potential victim. This becomes an even greater issue for MAPs and others dealing with Alcoholics and Drug Addicts. In 1987, 64 percent of all reported child abuse and neglect cases in New York City were associated with parental Alcohol and Other Drug abuse (Chasnoff, 1988). A study of 472 women by the Research Institute on Addictions in Buffalo, NY, found that 87 percent of alcoholic omen had been physically or sexually abused as children, compared to 59 percent of the nonalcoholic women surveyed (Miller and Downs, 1993). A 1993 study of more than 2,000 American couples found rates of domestic violence were almost 15 times higher in households where husbands were described as often drunk as opposed to never drunk (Collins and Messerschmidt, 1993). Battered women are at increased risk of attempting suicide, abusing alcohol and other drugs, depression, and abusing their own children (Fact Sheet on Physical and Sexual Abuse, 1993). Alcohol is present in more than 50 percent of all incidents of domestic violence. [5]

MAPs were always careful in protecting confidentiality. Locked offices and locked cabinets were the order of the day. Today many if not most use computers. We have to be doubly sure of safeguarding the records by using passwords, protecting from computer theft and other technical issues. We used posted letters which gave a large degree of confidentiality. Today e-mail is used, allowing confidential records to float in cyberspace. Safeguarding confidential information becomes more challenging and is protected by law.

Drug testing was addressed and involves various laws and the maintenance of the custody chain. There was no such thing as the Americans with Disabilities Act (ADA) or Family Medical Leave Act (FMLA). We had to learn and must keep up with these new protections. They are laws. Failing to adhere to these changes may lead to the MAP being sued. Malpractice Insurance is advised not only to protect the individual MAP but the entire organization.

We have come a long way and are still moving forward. The further we move forward the more laws we seem to come across, necessitating knowledge of applicable laws and keeping abreast of changes.

Conclusion

Alcohol has been around for thousands of years. There is mention of beer several times in the hieroglyphics of Ancient Egypt. Drinking alcohol is still going on and there is no sign that it will stop. It is both social and often religious. Many religions have alcohol in their rights. It is celebrated in the movies. We have seen all manner of Greek and Roman empire bacchanals. We have seen movies of Crusaders and Vikings drinking.. We have seen the tradition of the British Navy giving a ration of rum to the sailors. We have seen movies of WW II where soldiers and marines operate whiskey stills. Movies about the Viet Nam War openly depict and discuss drinking and the use of drugs. Alcohol and drugs are often mentioned in songs and song titles. As we headed toward the end of the 20th century, we have seen movies about drugs take a large place in the world of cinema. We have seen how drinking and drugging has been glorified and vilified, depending on the theme of a particular movie or song. Drugs and alcohol are a part of our every day life, real or imagined. Naturally, it is also a part of our work life. Work is a normal part of our lives. Some drink on the job, some off the job. Some drink in defiance of no-drinking on-the-job rules and some drink because drinking on-the-job is gently hinted at or often overtly encouraged. It has been used as a tool of management to increase production. When management does not approve of drinking, the rebelliousness of some workers comes to the fore. Drinking and drugging has taken an enormous toll on American industry and has for too many years. Something needed to be done and that something is helping the addict and alcoholic. It is often to the benefit of a company to help that sick person. The employer is beginning to look at an alcoholic or drug addict in the same light as he would view someone with diabetes or cancer. They are all diseases.

EAPs and MAPs may not be the only answer to the problem of drinking in the workplace but they area great start. Some kind of programs has been around for almost 200 years. These programs have become more professional in the past 50 years. Peer counselors from unions have been replaced by licensed counselors, many of whom are former peer counselors. Peer counseling is still an important part of assistance programs. The peer is often the first to notice a problem and often the first to let the individual know he or she is not alone and that there is help without condemnation. Assistance programs have not only survived they continue to grow both in numbers and in professionalism. There is a potpourri of acronyms out there indicating just how far assistance has come in the last half century. EAP, MAP, Certified Addiction Professional (CAP), National Certified Alcohol Counselor (NCAC), and Substance Abuse Professional (SAP) are just a few title denoting addiction counselors. The field also includes Social Workers, Psychiatrists, Psychologists and many other too numerous to mention. The field has grown and will continue to expand, numerically and professionally. The field now includes the previously mentioned Labor Assistance Professionals, the core of the Assistance Field. Their ranks include PhDs, Attorneys, Alcohol and Drug Counselors with numerous certifications, and almost any other degree one can imagine. Make no doubt about it; LAPs are professional in every way. They are dedicated, experienced and well educated and have access to expanded educational courses developed and directed at Unions Assistance Programs and the Workplace.

There are problems and people with problems. There are people willing and capable of helping. And when these helpers are in the work place they take on added tasks. They are often peers, counselors, friends, confidants. They are available to the employee or member. They are available to the family of the employee or member, often day, night, and weekends. They are knowledgeable, caring, and willing to help. For the most part, it does not cost them a penny. It is part of the company benefit package or a service offered by a union to the membership. They were needed in the past. They are needed today. They will be needed in the future. And they must continue to grow with the times.

Bibliography

Apgar, K., Burgess, A., <u>Working Solutions to Substance Abuse.</u>, (April 2001). Washington Business Group on Health, p. 2.

America's Fascinating Indian Heritage. (1978), <u>Reader's Digest,</u> p. 153.

Ames, G. (Fall 1989). <u>Alcohol-Related Movements and Their Effects on Drinking Policies in the American Workplace: An Historical Overview.</u> Journal of Drug Issues. p. 495.

Austin, Gregory A. *Alcohol in Western Society from Antiquity to 1800: A Chronological History.* Santa Barbara, CA: ABC — Clio, 1985.

Experts Debate Merits of Hair Testing for Drug Use. <u>Alcoholism and Drug Abuse Week.</u> (July, 29, 1996). p. 3.

Anderson, C. (June 1966). <u>Evaluation of the Acupuncture Program at the Kent/Sussex Detox Center.</u> Division of Management Services Delaware Health and Social Services.

Axelrod, L. (1995, Oct.). Positive Drug Test Results Decrease<u>. Management Review.</u> p 7.

Babor, Thomas. *Alcohol: Customs and Rituals.* New York: Chelsea House, 1986.

Bacharach, S., Bamberger, P., & Sonnenstuhl, W. (1994). <u>Member Assistance Programs in the Workplace</u>. Ithaca, New York: Cornell.

Bacharach, S., Bamberger, P., & Sonnenstuhl, W. (1996) MAPs: Labor-Based Peer Assistance in the Workplace. <u>Industrial Relations</u>, pp. 261-275.

Bahls, J. E. (1998, Feb.). Drugs in the Workplace. <u>H R Magazine</u>, pp. 81-87.

Balazs, Etienne. <u>Chinese Civilization and Bureaucracy.</u> New Haven, CT: Yale University Press, 1964. (Translated by H. M. Wright).

Bamberger, P. & Sonnenstuhl, W. (1995). Peer Referral Networks and Utilization of a Union-Based EAP. <u>The Journal of Drug Issues,</u> 25(2), pp. 291-312.

Bickerton, R. (1988). EAP's: Notes for a History in Progress. <u>Alcohol Health & Research World</u>, pp. 316-321.

Bickerton, R. (1990, November/December). Employee Assistance: A History in Progress. <u>EAP Digest</u>, pp. 34-42 & 82-84.

Boles, M. (Aug. 1997). <u>Blue Collar Worker Faces More Drug Tests. Workforce.</u> p.22.

Brown University Center for Alcohol and Addiction Studies, 2000, <u>Position Paper on Drug Policy, Physician Leadership on National Drug</u>

Bruhnsen, K. (1994, Aug.). Michigan Study Shows EAP Clients Use Less Sick Leave, Stay Longer. <u>EAPA Exchange</u>, pp. 11 & 27).

Blackmon, M. (1996, Jul.). Lessons From a Small Business Network. <u>Behavioral Health Management</u>, pp. 30-31.

Brady, T. (Feb. 1997). Bad hair Days,(Employee Drug Testing). <u>Management Review.</u> pp. 59 (3).

Braidwood, Robert J., Sauer, Jonathan D., Helbaek, Hans, Mangelsdorf, Paul C., Cutler, Hugh C., Coon, Careton S., Linton, Ralph, Steward, Julian, and Oppenheim, A. Leo. Symposium: Did man once live by beer alone? *American Anthropologist*, 1953, 55, 515-526.

Chandler, R. G., Kroeker, B. J., Flynn, M., and MacDonald, D. A. (1988). Evaluation of Employee Assistance Programs. M. J. Holosko and M. D. Feit (Eds.), <u>Establishing and Evaluating an</u>

Industrial Social Work Programme: The Seagram, Amherstburg Experience (pp. 243-253). New York-London: Haworth.

Chasnoff, I.J. (1988). Drugs, Alcohol, Pregnancy and Parenting. Northwestern University Medical School, Department of Pediatrics and Psychiatry and Behavioral Sciences. Hingham, MA, Kluwer Academic Publishers.

Cherrington, E. H.: The Evolution of Prohibition in The United States of America, Westerville, Ohio: American Issue Press (1920)

Cherrington, Ernest H. (Ed.) *Standard Encyclopedia of the Alcohol Problem*. 6 vols. Westerville, OH: American Issue Publishing Co., 1925-1930.

Collins, J.J., and Messerschmidt, M.A. Epidemiology of Alcohol-Related Violence. Alcohol Health and Reasearch World, 17(2):93-100. U.S. Department of Health and Human Services, National Institute on Alcohol Abuse and Alcoholism, 1993.

Curley, B. (April 21, 1997). Addiction insights Tells Us Where the Nation is Headed. Alcoholism and Drug Abuse Weekly, p. 5.

Daniels, S. (June 23, 1997). Drug Testing Cuts Costs and Accidents. National Underwriter (Property & Casualty/Risk & Benefits Management), p. 19.

de Bernardo, M. (1988). Drug Abuse in the Workplace: An Employer's Guide for Prevention, 2ed. Washington, DC.: U.S. Chamber of Commerce.

Dicks, B. A. (1988). Evaluation of Employee Assistance Programs. M. J. Holosko and M. D. Feit (Eds.), Evaluating the Development of Employee Assistance Programs in Rural Communities (pp. 255-264). New York-London: Haworth.

Drug Free Workplace Statistics: (9/21/2005). National Drug-Free Workplace Alliance:

Drugs in the Workplace. (1997). How EAPs Help Small Businesses Reduce Workers' Compensation Costs. Boston: Author.

Drug Use Among U.S. Workers: Prevalence and Trends by Occupation and Industry Categories. (1996, May). Rockville, MD: U.S. Department of Health and Human Services.

Fenn, D. (Feb. 1996). DOT Toughening up on Testing. Inc. p. 98.

Ferme Ghaliounqui, Paul. Fermented Beverages in Antiquity. In: Gastineau, Clifford F., Darby, William J., and Turner, Thomas B. (Eds.) Fermented Food Beverages in Nutrition. New York: Academic Press, 1979. Pp. 3-19.

Fact Sheet on Physical and Sexual Abuse, Substance Abuse and Mental Health Services Administration, April 1994

Franzese, R. A Review of the Reliability and Validity of the Addiction Severity Index. (Available from Accurate Assessments, PO Box 105, Boys Town, NE 68010.)

Flynn, G. (Apr. 1996). Will Drug Testing Pass or Fail in Court. Personnel Journal. pp. 141 (3).

Geber, S. (Aug. 1996), Corporate Burnout. Getting Results...for the Hands on Manager. pp. 8 (6).

Gemet, Jacques. Daily Life in China on the Eve of the Mongol Invasion 1250-1276. Stanford, CA: Stanford University Press, 1962. (Translated by H. M. Wright).

Gemignani, J. (Sept. 1996). Mental Health Matters. Business & Health. pp. 66.

Gemignani, J. (Feb. 1997). Targeting Substance Abuse. Business & Health. pp. 53-54.

Goff, V. & Young, S. (1996, Sept/Oct.). Improve Depression Management by Using Employment-Based Benefits and Services. EAP Association Exchange. pp. 14-15 & 39.

Gould, R. Focus: User Guide for Counselors & Therapists. (Available from Interactive Health Systems, 1337 Ocean Ave, Santa Monica, CA 90401).

Handron, K. (1994, April). Compensation for Stress, Employee Assistance.

Hart, Peter D. (1998). The Road to Recovery: A Landmark national Study on Public Perceptions of Alcoholism and Barriers to Treatment. Research Associates, Inc.

Hartwell, T., Steele, P. & Rodman, N (Nov., 1996). Prevalence of Drug Testing on the Workplace. Monthly Labor Review, pp. 35 (8).

Harvey, A. (1989). Local Action on Alcohol Problems. David Robinson, Philip Tether, and John Teller (Eds.), On the docks: awareness sessions with stevedores. pp. 99-103). London: Tavistock/Routledge.

Herm, G. (1975). The Celts. NY: St. Martin's Press.

Hess, F. (Sept 2, 1996). Fear in Corporate America. Industry Week, p. 25.

Intindola, B. (May 6, 1991), EAPs Still Foreign to Many Small Businesses. National Underwriter, p. 21.

Katz, S. H. and Voigt, M. M. Bread and beer: The early use of cereals in the human diet. Expedition, 1987, 28, 23-34.

Kinney, J., & Leaton, G. (1978). Loosening the Grip. St. Louis: C. V. Mosby.

Lee, F. C. (1988, Jul./Aug.). EAPs and managed care: A Blurring of the lines. EAP Digest, pp. 20 & 75.

Lender, M. & Martin, J. (1987). Drinking In America: A History. New York: the Free Press.

Lewis, D. C. (April, 1996). Random Drug Test in the Workplace Effective and Fair. The Brown University Digest of Addiction Theory and Application. pp. 1 (3).

Lucia, Salvatore P. *A History of Wine as Therapy*. Philadelphia, PA: J. B. Lippincott, 1963a.

Lausanne, Edita. *The Great Book of Wine*. New York: World Publishing Co., 1969.

Lutz, H. F. *Viticulture and Brewing in the Ancient Orient*. New York: J. C. Heinrichs, 1922.

Maiden, P. R. (1988). Evaluation of Employee Assistance Programs. M. J. Holosko and M. D. Feit (Eds.), Employee Assistance Program Evaluation in a Federal Government Agency (pp. 191-203). New York-London: Haworth.

Mark, F., Ph.D. (1989). Does Coercion Work? The Role of Referral Source in Motivating Alcoholics in Treatment. Alcoholism Treatment Quarterly, pp. 5-22.

Matching Alcoholism Treatment to Client Heterogeneity: Project MATCH Post treatment Drinking Outcomes. Rutgers University Center of Alcohol Studies, Rutgers:NJ.

McClellan, K. (1990, Vol. 5[4]). Early Intervention into Addictive and Mental Health Disorders. Employee Assistance Quarterly, pp. 71-82.

Mcdonald, S. & Springer, K. (Jul./Aug. 1998). Changes Ahead for SAP Regulations. EAPA Association Exchange, pp16-17.

McDonnell Douglas Corporation's EAP Produces Hard Data. (1989, Aug.). The Almacan, pp. 18-26.

Miller, B. and Downs, W. (1993). The Impact of Family Violence on the Use of Alcohol by Women. Alcohol and Health Research World, Vol. 17, No. 2, pp. 137-143.

Mitchell, J. & Everly, G. Jr. 1996, Critical Incident Stress Management: The Basic Sourse Workbook. International Critical Incident Stress Foundation, Inc., Ellicott City, MD, p. 28.

Monckton, Herbert A. *A History of English Ale and Beer*. London: Bodley Head, 1966.

Morton, R. (Jan. 1997). Time to Tweak the Testing Rules. Transportation & Distribution. pp. 68 & 70.

National Drug Control Strategy, 1997. (1997). Washington, DC: U.S. Government Printing Office.

National Household Survey on Drug Abuse: Main Findings 1994. (1994). Rockville, MD: U.S. Department of Health and Human Services.

National Household Survey on Drug Abuse: Population Estimates 1995. (1995). Rockville, MD: U.S. Department of Health and Human Services.

National Household Survey on Drug Abuse, 2000. (9/6/2002). Substance use, Dependence or Abuse Among Full-time Workers. Rockville, MD: U.S. Department of Health and Human Services.

National Household Survey on Drug Abuse, 2000. (9/27/2002). Awareness of Workplace Substance Use Policies and Programs. Rockville, MD: U.S. Department of Health and Human Services.

National Household Survey on Drug Abuse, 2001. (4/2/2004). Employed Admissions: 2001. Rockville, MD: U.S. Department of Health and Human Services.

National Underwriter. (Apr. 4, 1994. Few Substance Abusers are found in Drug Tests. p. 7.

Patrick, Charles H. *Alcohol, Culture, and Society*. Durham, NC: Duke University Press, 1952. Reprint edition by AMS Press, New York, 1970.

Peck, R. (1995, Mar.-Apr.). Computerized Reports: What Employers Want. Behavioral Health Management, pp. 32[2].

Pontius, P. The EAP Manual: An Information Guide to Implementing and Maintaining an Employee Assistance Program in the Workplace. The Business Council of New York State, Inc. p., 1.

Practical Approaches in the Treatment of Women Who Abuse Alcohol and Other Drugs. (1994). Rockville, MD: U.S. Department of Health and Human Services.

Preliminary Estimates from the National Household Survey on Drug Abuse. (1996, Aug.). Rockville, MD: U.S. Department of Health and Human Services.

Preliminary Estimates from the National Household Survey on Drug Abuse. (1997, Jul.). Raymond, Irving W. *The Teaching of the Early Church on the Use of Wine and Strong Drink*. New York: Columbia University Press, 1927.

Robbins, Tom. Labor's Loneliest Battles (May 23—29, 2001). The Village Voice.

Roman, P. & Blum, T., Ph.Ds (1989). Alcohol Problem Intervention in the Workplace. Alcohol Health & Research World, pp. 375-380.

Rorabaugh, W. J. *The Alcholic Republic, an American Tradition* New York: Oxford University Press, 1979

Scanlon, W. (1991). Alcoholism and Drug Abuse in the Workplace: Managing Care and Costs Through Employee Assistance Programs. (2nd ed.). New York: Praeger.

Schiff, L. (Nov. 1997). Downsizing Workplace Stress. Business and Health, pp. 45-46.

Seventh Special Report to the U.S. Congress on Alcohol and Health. (1990). Rockville, MD: U.S. Department of Health and Human Services.

Seventh Special Report to the U.S. Congress on Alcohol and Health, 1990. Rockville, MD: U.S. Department of Health and Human Services.

Simms. L. (1988, July/August). Managed Health Care: What It Is and How It Works. EAP Digest, pp. 32-38 & 63-74.

Sinclair, B. (March, 1996). New DOT Drug and Alcohol Regulations. Beverage Industry. pp. 45 (2).

Smith, M. (May 21, 1993). Testimony presented to the NIH Office of Alternative Medicine and the National Wellness Coalition). (Available from National Acupuncture Detoxification Association, PO Box 1927, Vancouver, WA. 98668).

Sonnenstuhl, W. & Trice, H. (1986). Strategies For Employee Assistance Programs. The Crucial Balance. New York: Cornell University.

Sonnenstuhl, W. & Trice, H. (1987). The Social Construction of Alcohol Problems in a Union's Peer Counseling Program. The Journal of Drug Issues, 17(3), 223-254.

Steele, P. (Spring 1995). Worker Assistance Programs and Labor Process: Emergence and Development of Employee Assistance Model. Journal of Drug Issues. p. 430.

Sternberg, D., M. D.(1989). Dual Diagnosis: Addiction and Affective Disorders. The Psychiatric Hospital, Vol.20/NO.2, pp. 71-77).

Stone, Florence (Dec. 1997). Why Are Today's Workers Stressed Out. Getting Results...for the Hands-On Manager, p.1.

Supreme Court Could Usher In A Wave of Drug Testing (Oct, 13, 1997), Alcohol and Drug Abuse Week. pp1 (2).

Thormann, K. ((1996, Mar.-Apr.). Customized Care Can Be Cost Effective. Behavioral Health Management, pp. 18[4].

Unites States Department of Human Services: 22 MILLION IN U.S. SUFFER FROM SUBSTANCE DEPENDENCE OR ABUSE: (9/2/03).

Verespej, M. (Feb. 17, 1992). Drug Users — Not Testing — Anger Workers. Industry Week. pp. 33-34. Wallace, A. F. (1972). The Death and Rebirth of the Seneca. New York: Vintage

Winick, C., Ph.D. (1985) Starting an Employee Assistance Program: A Guide for Councils and Unions. New York: AFL/CIO.

Wise, D. (Apr. 1993). Employee Assistance Programs Expand to Fit Companies' Needs. Business & Health, pp. 40 (5).

Wrich, J. (Sept. 1996). Brief Summary of Audit Findings of Managed Behavioral Health Care Services submitted to The Congressional Budget Office.

Wright, D. A. (1988). Evaluation of Employee Assistance Programs. M. J. Holosko and M. D. Feit (Eds.), A Brief Overview of Research Techniques Used to Evaluate Three Employee Assistance Programs Through the Family Service Association of Metropolitan Toronto Experience (pp. 205-210). New York-London: Haworth.

Young, N., Ph.D. (1994). Invest in Treatment for Alcohol and Other Drugs: It Pays. University of California Los Angeles, School of Public Policy and Social Research, Department of Social Welfare.

Zweben, J., Ph.D. (1987, Apr.-Jun.). Eating Disorders and Substance Abuse. Journal of Psychoactive Drugs, 19(2), 181-192.

Reference Web Sites

Does Drug Use by Workers Really Reduce Productivity? http://www.hrmguide.net/usa/health/drug_use_by_workers.htm

Drug Guide By Slang: www.drugfree.org/portal/drug_guide/BySlang

History of Alcohol and Drinking Around the World: David J. Hanson, Ph.D. (http://www2.potsdam.edu/hansondj/Controversies/1114796842.html

Substance Abuse in the Workplace, A Dangerous and Expensive Problem: http://alcoholism.about.com/cs/work/a/aa990120.htm

Temperance: http://64.1911encyclopedia.org/T/TE/TEMPERANCE.htm

The Substance Abuse Costs to Society & Workplaces Are Huge http://www.drug-addiction.com/drugs_at_work.htm

http://susanbanthonyhouse.org/biography.shtml#LABACT

Women's Christian Temperance Movement: (Spring, 2000), Roberts, http://religiousmovements.lib.virginia.edu/nrms/wctu.html

http://earlyamerica.com/review/2002_summer_fall/forefathers.htm

http://www.jcs-group.com/cruisin/booze/alcohol.html

http://www.nida.nih.gov/Infofacts/clubdrugs.html

http://www.druglibrary.org/schaffer/Library/studies/nc/nc2a.htm (*)

http://store.health.org/catalog/facts.aspx?topic=3 (*)

http://www.ensuringsolutions.org/pages/refash.html#4 (*)

http://www.alcoholismcures.com/alcohol/alcohol_history.html

http://www.whitehousedrugpolicy.gov/drugfact/cocaine/index.html

http://dl.lib.brown.edu/temperance/rhetoric.html

http://www.hopenetworks.org/OverviewCostsAlcohol.html

www.ingramcontent.com/pod-product-compliance
Lightning Source LLC
Chambersburg PA
CBHW060458290526
45791CB00001B/167